LENDING POLICY

IF YOU DAMAGE OR LOSE LIBRARY
MATERIALS, THEN YOU WILL BE
CHARGED FOR REPLACEMENT. FAIL-
URE TO PAY AFFECTS LIBRARY
PRIVILEGES, GRADES, TRANSCRIPTS,
DIPLOMAS, AND REGISTRATION
PRIVILEGES OR ANY COMBINATION
THEREOF.

MAY 20 '92

Why Blacks, Women, and Jews Are Not Mentioned in the Constitution, and other unorthodox views

Why Blacks, Women, and Jews Are Not Mentioned in the Constitution, and other unorthodox views

Robert A. Goldwin

With a Foreword by Edwin M. Yoder, Jr.,
Pulitzer Prize–Winning Columnist

The AEI Press
Publisher for the American Enterprise Institute
Washington, D.C.

Distributed by arrangement with

National Book Network
4720 Boston Way   3 Henrietta Street
Lanham, MD 20706   London WC2E 8LU England

Library of Congress Cataloging-in-Publication Data

Goldwin, Robert A., 1922–
    Why Blacks, women and Jews are not mentioned in the Constitution,
and other unorthodox views / Robert A. Goldwin.
        p.   cm. — (AEI studies ; 494)
    ISBN 0-8447-3693-7 (alk. paper)

    1. Civil rights—United States—History.   2. United States-
-Constitutional history.   I. Title.   II. Series.
KF4749.A2G65   1989
342.73'085—dc20
[347.30285]   89-17658
                                                                   CIP

AEI Studies 494

The AEI Press
Publishers for the American Enterprise Institute
1150 17th Street, N.W., Washington, D.C. 20036

Printed in the United States of America

To Daisy

Contents

Foreword

Philosopher kings and platonic guardians are out of fashion in politics today, and no wonder. Visionary governance, claiming to draw a mandate from the eternal order of things, has developed an unsavory reputation in our century. Some of it has been singularly cruel.

But this chastening fact does not rid us of the need for political philosophizing and may actually increase it. The question is, What kind of philosophizing? The essays of Robert Goldwin are the right kind in my book. They encourage me to think that political philosophy has a future. Certainly rulers counseled by Goldwin would rule benevolently and wisely. They would be neither wreckers of hallowed custom nor slaves to it. Custom would be constantly tested for congruency with the principles of Madison, Locke, and other great thinkers of the democratic tradition. This continuing dialogue on the first principles of the good society would not be an airy abstraction either. It would have its footing on solid ground. It would be in touch with the texture of life, with the evolving economic order, with the state of technology, with the availability of resources. But there would be no flaccid relativism about it. It would honor the belief of the framers that they were exhibiting man's capacity to design a government rather than accept what accident decreed.

All the essays gathered here make good reading. But two stand out and would glitter in any anthology of memorable writing in the field of political theory. One is the title essay, with which Goldwin pronounces himself "least dissatisfied." The other is "Locke and the Law of the Sea," a piece that had a demonstrable effect on policy at a crucial juncture of U.S. treaty making. Both essays display, in heightened form, the qualities that make Goldwin an influential essayist.

In "Why Blacks, Women, and Jews Are Not Mentioned in the Constitution," Goldwin's target is perhaps that self-flagellating, often utterly unhistorical kind of speechifying that sells the Constitution short, which ritually deplores it as a time-bound eighteenth-century document framed by a small white male elite for its own convenience.

Edwin M. Yoder is a Rhodes Scholar, Pulitzer Prize–winning editorial writer, and nationally syndicated political columnist.

No one with a grain of history or common sense in his bones can possibly believe this libel. Yet it has been a surprisingly persistent theme in the national conversation. In modern times, it goes back at least to Charles A. Beard, and he was hardly its first spokesman. The progressive Beard has had imitators of other persuasions, even in the bicentennial season. The theme is drearily familiar. In how many speeches has it been lamented that the framers lacked our own large vision of social compassion and inclusiveness? Too many, all exhibiting the bad American habit of patronizing the past. Anyone tempted by that version of the events of 1787 should examine Goldwin's argument as a corrective. By the simple trick of examining what the text actually says (and, as important, does not say), Goldwin persuasively establishes that the framers were far wiser than their critics think: wise enough to style their language, as they did the great rules of representative government, with an eye to a future whose contours they could only guess at.

They hoped they were designing a durable government for that "empire of liberty" of which Jefferson spoke, capable of continental expansion. So they wrote a document to match, one whose language would have the elasticity of understatement, a capacity to absorb great change without strain or embellishment. It is further proof, perhaps, that the framers were not "morally greedy," to use one of Goldwin's favorite phrases. They did not fancy they were designing a form of government to be operated for or by angels. They relied on rival ambitions and "factions" to check and offset the imperious urges of one another. This was not cynicism; it was moral and political modesty.

Likewise, the essay entitled "Locke and the Law of the Sea" teaches us to see more plainly what is there to be seen. As a student of Locke, Goldwin was not enthralled by the high-flown rhetoric about the "common heritage of mankind." He knew in what sense it was correct, in what sense incorrect, to analogize the sea and the seabed to a village common fixed by custom and positive law. Here, the political philosopher serves his society well, rescuing the rest of us from muddle or mesmeric ideological fashion.

Both these memorable essays, and others in this collection as well, prove all over again that ideas have consequences and that they are often large ones. But that was always the case. "Indeed," as Lord Keynes wrote in that memorable passage near the end of his *General Theory*, "the world is ruled by little else. . . . Madmen in authority, who hear voices in the air, are distilling their frenzy from some academic scribbler of a few years back." True indeed—but if so, how do we distinguish one scribbler from another, a sound thinker from one whose fevered musings ignite the frenzies of zealots and madmen? There is finally no other test, certainly none more reliable, than real consequences. Look around. See whose ideas have served the peace, security, and happiness of man and whose have robbed him of sleep and even life.

There is no danger of unwholesome result here. Robert Goldwin is devoted to the traditions of individual liberty and democracy; an unwholesome frenzy arising from his writings is unimaginable. In Washington, he is known not only as an essayist but as a cheerful and courteous mentor, the primary organizer of the decade-long Constitution Project at AEI. As an occasional participant in the resulting seminars, I doubt that they had many rivals for depth, seriousness, and interest. Indeed, if everyone had Bob Goldwin as a teacher, there would be less muddle and ignorance of the kind he discusses in "What Americans Know about Their Constitution." There would be less idle pedantry as well; for with typical second thought, Goldwin observes that if the ideas are sound, that matters far more than mistaken notions as to where in the framing documents they may be found. The ideas are the vital essence, for good or ill, and grasping those essences is what political theory at its best is all about. It is a skill that Robert Goldwin practices with the best.

EDWIN M. YODER, JR.

1
Principles and Politics—
An Introduction

Many years after he wrote the Declaration of Independence, Thomas Jefferson undertook to respond to criticisms of his authorship of that renowned and revered American founding document. The criticisms were all variations on one point, the Declaration's lack of originality: there were no new ideas in it (Thomas Pickering), the ideas that were in it were commonplaces that "had been hackneyed in Congress two years before" (John Adams), and it was all just copied from John Locke's treatise on government (Richard Henry Lee).[1]

Jefferson's response was an explanation, not a denial. "The object of the Declaration of Independence," he wrote in 1825, the year before his death, in a letter to Henry Lee,

> was not to find out new principles, or new arguments, never before thought of, not merely to say things which had never been said before; but to place before mankind the common sense of the subject. . . . Neither aiming at originality of principle or sentiment, nor yet copied from any particular and previous writing, it was intended to be an expression of the American mind. . . . All its authority rests then on the harmonizing sentiments of the day, whether expressed in conversation, in letters, printed essays, or in the elementary books of public right, as Aristotle, Cicero, Locke, Sidney, &c.[2]

In short, the critics' assertions were true, but beside the point. What we learn authoritatively from Jefferson is that the founding American ideas had their origins in other nations and other times and are not original with Americans. What he sought to express was what Americans were thinking, saying, writing, and reading at that time. But if a knowledgeable contemporary could read this "expression of the American mind" and think that it was copied out of Locke's treatise on government, it seems clear that Locke's thought had been so completely absorbed by Americans of the time that it could be considered "the common sense of the subject." Jefferson's own list of the sources of American founding ideas was broader: not only Locke,

1

but also Aristotle, Cicero, Sidney, and others. Whatever claims might be made for invention, innovation, and originality in the American founding—and they are many—we have Jefferson's own testimony that such claims cannot be made with respect to the founding principles.

The American founding principles are that the people themselves are the true source of political power, that no one can be justly governed without his own consent, that all human beings are equal in their natural rights to life and liberty, and that the principal purpose of governments is to secure individual rights. All of these were written by Locke and others before the United States came into being. The great American achievement was to adopt them as living principles of political action and make them the foundation of an entirely new kind of nation.

To admit, as Jefferson does, that the principles were not new in no way contradicts the proud assertion of James Madison that the people of the United States "accomplished a revolution which has no parallel in the annals of human society." Madison agreed that the ideas were drawn from "former times and other nations," but the true innovation, the unprecedented achievement was that on borrowed principles "they reared the fabrics of governments which have no model on the face of the globe."[3]

Policy and principles are invariably linked in the American experience, more so than in the case of most nations, because the United States is a founded nation, founded, as Alexander Hamilton said, by "reflection and choice" rather than by "accident and force."[4] American principles are not always obvious but they can be discovered. That discovery, however, can only begin the quest. The next essential steps are to discover how the principles are linked to political practice. That is the underlying and guiding quest that gives unity to the essays in this book: the effort to identify and understand the fundamental principles as evidenced in American institutions, American character, and American policies.

We Americans pride ourselves on being practical-minded. Philosophical reflection does not come easily to us. But if we want to think well about our political system we have no choice in the matter. To understand ourselves we must understand our principles, and to understand the principles we must go far afield in tracing them to their original, foreign sources. Only by the effort to see America in that broad context can we achieve full understanding of who we are, where we came from, how we got where we are, and where we should be going as a nation and a people.

Much of what I have written results from my studies with Professor Leo Strauss, who taught me more than I know. He is the one teacher to whom I am most indebted. By the power of example, he inclined students to be disciplined in their reading, unprejudiced when confronted with unfamiliar or unorthodox teachings, and on guard against all dogma and unexamined doctrine, whether of others or their own. Much of the rest I learned from friends and colleagues—the late Martin Diamond and Herbert Storing, Walter Berns, Joseph Cropsey, and Edward Banfield. A difficulty I have as a result of my good fortune in these instructors is that I can no longer discern what I have appropriated rather directly from them and what I have discovered for myself. I am willing to give to them all the credit they deserve for almost any of these thoughts; the trouble is that I cannot be sure whom to credit for what.

I know I have not read everything written about my subjects, so I cannot say and do not say that some of these things have not been written before. The distinctions I make are what I know I learned from others, what I may have learned from others and can no longer distinguish from my own discoveries, and, finally, what I think is my own original thought I claim as my own, for instance, the idea that certain silences in the Constitution are significant; the title essay in this book, the one of all my essays that dissatisfies me the least, is a lesson in how to read the Constitution on subjects it doesn't mention.

I know that I learned from Walter Berns and Herbert Storing the fundamental importance of the difference between studying the Constitution and studying constitutional law. Most of what I have to say in this volume about the Constitution is drawn from thinking about the Constitution itself and not about what the Supreme Court says, or fails to say, about the Constitution. This means regarding the Constitution as the framework of our government and of our political society more than as a legal document. The first provision of the Constitution is that the Congress shall consist of a Senate and House of Representatives. For anyone who seeks to understand American government, it is a fact of great importance that we have two chambers of different sizes, elected on different principles of representation, with different lengths of terms, with different rules and different constitutional powers. Serious study of the Constitution directs one's attention to the consequences of having such a bicameral national legislature. But no such attention is required in studying constitutional law, because the bicameral character of the Congress has been of minimal importance in litigation and therefore almost never, if ever, a factor in cases before the courts.

Study of constitutional law leads to consideration above all of provisions of the Constitution that are unclear in themselves or in their application to unforeseen controversies. Study of the Constitution leads to consideration of provisions that may never be the subject

3

of litigation but may nevertheless be fundamental to an understanding of the way the American people have constituted themselves politically, economically, and socially. The essays in this volume are studies of the Constitution, not of constitutional law.

I am sure that I did not learn from someone else the importance of the hidden design of Madison's list of rights when he, more than a little unwillingly, did get around to proposing them. Madison did not call his proposed amendments a bill of rights. What we call the Bill of Rights was something new that Madison invented, unlike any previous bill of rights. My view is that it has worked so well because of its novel Madisonian features. I would be gratified, indeed, if one day people gave the name of "Goldwin's rule" to the phenomenon that rights have been most secure where the constitutional list of rights is short, negative, free of guarantees, and not linked to duties.

I feel confident that I worked out for myself the distinction between righteousness and self-righteousness in my search for morality in the Constitution; I even know the erstwhile friend, from whom I learned so much in earlier days, and for whom I now have diminished respect and no affection, who was the living model in my mind as I thought through the ugly consequences of the descent from righteous principles to all-consuming self-righteousness.

It will be obvious to readers that I have been instructed and influenced by my long study of Locke, but I am ambivalent on the question of whether to consider myself a Lockean. To put it too briefly and sweepingly, much of what we deplore in modern American life—the poverty of spirit, the excessive concern for comfort and convenience, the emphasis on self and selfishness—can be ascribed to Locke, sometimes to his true teaching, more often to a distortion of it. Much of what is most admirable in human nature, and most noble in social and political life, is slighted by Locke, or denied. I once described him as "a backwards Midas": golden things he touched turned to iron.

The paradox is that we also owe to Locke much of our enjoyment of the best fruits of modernity. Nations that have been taught by Locke are freer, more stable, more prosperous, more peaceable, and more successful in providing security for the rights of every individual. And Lockean nations—that is, nations whose first principles are liberty and equality of rights—never go to war against each other. That accounts for my ambivalence; it is hard to be a Lockean and equally hard, for an American, not to be one.

For several years I had the opportunity to live the task of applying principle to policy. I served in Brussels as adviser to the U.S. ambassador to the North Atlantic Treaty Organization (NATO), in the White House as special consultant to the president, and in the Pentagon as adviser to the secretary of defense, but the greatest influence I ever had on policy occurred after I had become a private citizen again, as a result of publication of the essay, "Locke and the Law of the Sea." Soon after its appearance I was asked to serve as a consultant to the Law of the Sea Office in the Pentagon, to serve on the State Department's Advisory Committee on the Law of the Sea, and to provide talking points for the president's special emissary to heads of government to persuade them to stand with the United States in opposition to the deep seabed provisions of the treaty. President Reagan took the first step very early in his presidency by halting progress toward rapid approval of the treaty, but his problem was that the diplomats who were most knowledgeable about the treaty were, almost without exception, strongly committed to approval of the treaty they had worked on for so many years; those who saw the follies of its deep seabed provisions and wanted to support the president's stand needed sound and persuasive arguments. Locke provided them.

It was apparent to a student of Locke that "the common heritage of mankind," the theoretical basis of the treaty, was a flimsy, confused, upside-down version of a state-of-nature teaching; it needed only a slight push to collapse of its own weighty nonsense. The article provided that push and, in the end, the treaty sank, although, sad to say, the defeated international diplomats still persevere in their efforts to apply "the common heritage of mankind" principle to something, if not to manganese nodules at the bottom of the sea, then to the geostationary orbit in outer space, to the moon, to Antarctica, or to anything unowned that they might claim, supposedly in the name of all mankind, as international property subject to their regulation. They have not yet succeeded, but they keep on trying. This experience of successful application of principle to practice through publication, however, has greatly strengthened my appreciation of the power of the pen.

There can be no doubt of the source of all my ideas on liberal education. They came to me through my years of association with St. John's College in Annapolis, the justly famous Great Books school, first as an undergraduate and later as a teaching member of the faculty and dean. I learned from the books and from the teaching faculty, first as their student, then as a colleague. Others have made the case that the state of higher education in the United States is deplorable, and I do not disagree; but in my opinion there are small enclaves of excellence on just about every college or university campus, one or a few devoted and thoughtful professors who make it possible for a serious student, with some luck, to get a good education. St. John's College is, however, the only campus I know that is itself, in its entirety, just such an enclave.

One of the grave troubles with institutions of undergraduate

5

education is that they are dominated by the graduate schools' narrow specializations, which are antithetical to sound general or liberal education. The teaching faculty of most undergraduate departments are men and women who take their bearings from their training in graduate school, their own subsequent research in a specialized field, and their intention to prepare students for graduate study. As a consequence, they have a distorted view of what college education ought to be. The courses of study are rarely appropriate except as preliminary to more advanced study.

For example, if all freshmen are required to take one introductory course in political science, what should they be asked to study? For many years most undergraduate political science departments offered "the methodology of the social sciences" as their introductory course. They seemed to consider training for a career as a professional political scientist as the first priority for undergraduates. But wouldn't it be more sensible to ask them to study politics from the viewpoint of the active citizen, rather than methodology from the viewpoint of the professional social scientist? That is, since hardly any of them will or should become professional social scientists, doesn't it make better educational sense to insist that they read the best books on the universal problems inherent in the efforts of human beings, all over the world and down through the ages, to organize themselves for the purpose of living well together in political communities?

It is rare for any undergraduate faculty to ask the obvious question, "What should undergraduates study?" The founders of the present St. John's College curriculum were unusual if not unique in that respect; they not only asked that question fifty years ago, they answered it exceedingly well. My hope is that what is said in this book about liberal education reflects in some measure the qualities of extraordinary teachers like Jacob Klein, Simon Kaplan, and Richard Scofield and of other unsung giants of the St. John's College classrooms. Those classrooms continue to be enclaves of excellence, fully in accord with the spirit of our constitutional republic and the best practice of the republic of letters.

Finally, I acknowledge my gratitude to the American Enterprise Institute for Public Policy Research, an organization devoted to studying principles and the complexities of applying them in practice. There could not be a more suitable home for my studies, or more congenial and helpful colleagues. Happy chance brought me to AEI. And as all students of politics know, though hard work is necessary, it sure helps to be lucky.

PART ONE

The Constitution—
Old Ideas in a New Order

2
Why Blacks, Women, and Jews Are Not Mentioned in the Constitution

The bicentennial we celebrated in 1987 honored the Constitution written in 1787, that is, the original, unamended Constitution. Some well-meaning citizens denounced celebrating or even praising that Constitution. They contended that its many severe defects should be considered a matter of national shame. For example, lacking the Thirteenth Amendment, the original Constitution permitted slavery to continue; lacking the Nineteenth Amendment, it did not secure the right of women to vote; and, lacking the First Amendment, it provided no protection for religious freedom, not to mention other rights. Why, they ask, should we celebrate a constitution that treated blacks as less than human, that left women out, and that did not combat religious intolerance?

These charges would be distressing if true, but fortunately they are false. They stem from a misreading of the document, a misreading that comes from not appreciating the importance of knowing how to read the original Constitution on subjects it does not mention.

Why bother with subjects not mentioned? Because we have no choice. The list of unusually important subjects the Constitution does not mention is very long. The fact that they are not mentioned has not prevented cases and controversies from arising, nor has it relieved courts and legislatures of the duty of determining what is constitutional with regard to them. The words "education" and "school," for example, do not occur in the Constitution, but even so the courts have been busy for decades deciding school controversies. There is no mention of labor unions, corporations, political parties, the air force, radio and television broadcasting, telecommunications, and so on, but the courts deliberate constitutional controversies on these subjects all the time. The list of subjects not mentioned in the text of the Constitution also includes words like "abortion," "contraceptives," and "sodomy" and phrases like "right to privacy," "substantive due process," "separation of powers," and the "high wall separating church and state"—all matters on which the Supreme Court has pronounced.

The inescapable fact is that many subjects not mentioned in the Constitution must be interpreted, unavoidably, by anyone for whom the meaning of the Constitution is important. My argument is that there are valuable lessons to be learned about how we are constituted as a nation and what in the original Constitution is worth celebrating, by devoting serious attention to subjects not mentioned in it. For that purpose, I propose close attention to three such subjects—blacks, women, and Jews.

Blacks

What to do about black slavery was a major concern in the Constitutional Convention; it was discussed at length in the debates, with frequent direct reference to both slavery and race. But neither term was mentioned when it came to the writing. No words indicating race or color, black or white, occur in the text of the Constitution, and neither do the words "slave" or "slavery." Circumlocutions are used in the text to avoid the use of any form of the word "slave": for example, "person held to service or labor," and "such persons as any of the States now existing shall think proper to admit."

In fact, the word "slavery" entered the Constitution for the first time after the Civil War, in the Thirteenth Amendment, which thereafter prohibited slavery anywhere in the United States. The words "race" and "color" were first used in the Fifteenth Amendment for the purpose of securing the right of all citizens to vote. The words "black" and "white" have never been part of the Constitution.

What difference does it make, one may well ask, that the words were not used, if the ugly fact is that black slavery existed and was given constitutional status? Consider, for example, perhaps the most notorious and most misunderstood constitutional provision relating to black slavery, the famous "three-fifths clause."

As Benjamin Hooks, executive director of the National Association for the Advancement of Colored People, put it in criticism of the original Constitution: "Article I, section 2, clause 3 of the Constitution itself starts off with a quota: three-fifths. That is how folks were counted in that original Constitution." That provision, Hooks said, "establishes black folk—they did not call us that, they had a very good way of saying it—as three-fifths of a person."[1] Hooks is not alone in this view. The historian John Hope Franklin has written of this same clause that the founders "degraded the human spirit by equating five black men with three white men";[2] and the constitutional law professor Lino Graglia contends that the provision "that a slave was to be counted as three-fifths of a free person for purposes of representation" shows "how little the Constitution had to do with aspirations for brotherhood or human dignity."[3]

These three agree in expressing the widely held view of this clause that, for the founders, blacks were less than human, somehow or other only a fraction of a human being. The constitutional clause they are referring to reads as follows:

> Representatives and direct taxes shall be apportioned among the several States . . . according to their respective numbers, which shall be determined by adding to the whole number of free persons, including those bound to service for a term of years, and excluding Indians not taxed, three-fifths of all other persons.

In short, count all of the free persons and indentured servants, do not count the Indians, and then add three-fifths of the slaves. The question is what, if anything, does that provision tell us about what the founders thought about slavery and about blacks as blacks and as human beings?

James Madison said in the convention that slavery was the central problem. Southern delegates emphasized that there was no chance of union including the South without accepting the long-established existence of slavery in the slaveholding states. But slavery was a flat contradiction of the principles of the Declaration of Independence, the principles that are the bedrock of the Constitution—the primacy of the rights of individuals, their equality with respect to their rights, and the consequence that the consent of the governed is the only legitimate source of political power. Almost all the delegates were fully aware that slavery profoundly contradicted these principles and therefore had no proper place in the Constitution.

If on the one hand the continuation of slavery was unavoidable, and on the other hand it was a contradiction of the most fundamental principles of the Constitution the delegates wanted and thought necessary, what could principled antislavery delegates do? One effective and consistent thing they could do was try to make the political base of slavery as weak as possible, to diminish its influence and improve the chances of eradicating it some time in the future.

The struggle that took place in the convention was between Southern delegates trying to strengthen the constitutional supports for slavery and Northern delegates trying to weaken them. That issue—the initial and subsequent political strength of slavery—was in contention on the question of representation in the House of Representatives. It was agreed that every state, regardless of size, would have two senators. But the number of representatives from any state would be apportioned according to its population, and that raised the question of whom to include in the count.

Slave-state delegates were in favor of including every slave, just as they would any other inhabitant. Madison's notes indicate that the delegates from South Carolina "insisted that blacks be included in the rule of representation, equally with the Whites."

On the other side, delegates from the nonslave states were opposed to counting the slaves, because it would give the South more votes and because it made a mockery of the principle of representation to count persons who had no influence whatsoever on the lawmaking process and who therefore were not "represented" in the legislature in any meaningful sense of the word. Counting the slaves for purposes of representation would also give the slave states an incentive to increase their slave population instead of decreasing it. In short, considering the chief purpose of this clause in the Constitution, it is obvious that an antislavery delegate would not want to count the slaves at all.

In the end, two things were done. First, it was agreed to use the census for two opposed purposes: representation and direct taxation. As the count of persons went up in any state, seats in Congress and direct taxes to be paid went up as well; as the count of persons went down, both the number of Congressmen and the direct taxes to be paid went down. Combining these two, and thereby establishing opposing incentives, seems clearly intended to provide a restraint on a state's either getting too much representation or avoiding paying a fair share of direct taxes. The additional compromise was that three-fifths of the slaves would be included in the population count, as the alternative to including all or none.

If none of the slaves had been included, as Northern delegates wanted, the slave states would have had only 41 percent of the seats in the House. If all of the slaves had been included, as Southerners wanted, the slave states would have had 50 percent of the seats. By agreeing to include three-fifths of them, the slave states ended up with 47 percent—not negligible, but still a minority likely to be outvoted on slavery issues.[4]

However the slavery provisions look to us today, they had to be explained to concerned citizens in the South as well as the North. Charles Pinckney reported to the South Carolina ratifying convention that he thought they had "made the best terms for the security of [slavery] it was in our power to make. We would have made better if we could, but on the whole, I do not think them bad." At the same time, Northern delegates were saying the opposite in a very similar fashion. James Wilson reported to the Pennsylvania ratifying convention that he thought they had succeeded in "laying the foundation for banishing slavery out of this country," but he regretted that "the period is more distant than I could wish."

In brief, both North and South, in trying to weaken or strengthen slavery, had sought more and gotten less than each had wanted, but for the sake of union had accepted a result that was "not bad."

The struggle between proslavery and antislavery forces for control of Congress, begun in the Constitutional Convention and continued relentlessly for more than seventy years thereafter, was the major cause of the Civil War and persisted long after that war and the constitutional amendments that followed it had ended slavery.

But to understand what the original Constitution had to say about blacks, the point is that the three-fifths clause had nothing at all to do with measuring the human worth of blacks. *Northern* delegates did not want black slaves included, not because they thought them unworthy of being counted, but because they wanted to weaken the slaveholding power in Congress. *Southern* delegates wanted every slave to count "equally with the Whites," not because they wanted to proclaim that black slaves were human beings on an equal footing with free white persons, but because they wanted to increase the proslavery voting power in Congress. The humanity of blacks was not the subject of the three-fifths clause; voting power in Congress was the subject.

Thus, the three-fifths clause is irrelevant to the question of what the founders thought of the slaves as human beings. What is relevant are two indisputable facts: in the original Constitution there is no mention of color, race, or slavery, and nowhere in it are slaves called anything but "persons."

There is nothing new in the point that the original Constitution does not mention slavery. Luther Martin, a Maryland delegate to the Constitutional Convention who opposed ratification, explained to the Maryland legislature in 1787 that the authors of the Constitution did not use the word slave because they "anxiously sought to avoid the admission of expressions which might be odious in the ears of Americans."[5] And the great black leader and orator Frederick Douglass commented on this silence in 1852, arguing against the "slander" on the memory of the founders that the original Constitution was proslavery. "In that instrument," he said, "I hold there is neither warrant, license, nor sanction of the hateful thing." And a major element of his evidence is that "neither *slavery, slaveholding,* nor *slave* can anywhere

13

be found in it. . . . Now, take the Constitution according to its plain reading, and I defy the presentation of a single pro-slavery clause in it."[6]

These two very different speakers, Luther Martin and Frederick Douglass, knew this fact about the silence of the Constitution about slavery, and so did many, many others. But apparently it needed to be pointed out in their times, and it needs to be pointed out today. And especially when we recall that there is an equal silence about race, do we see the importance of reminding ourselves about this point that seems to have been forgotten or persistently ignored by most Americans, even by unusually knowledgeable ones like Benjamin Hooks and John Hope Franklin.

Despite the existence of slavery and the persistence of it for seventy-five years more, the founders left us with a constitutional document that has accommodated a very different order of things with regard to the place in our society of the descendants of former slaves. I do not contend that delegates foresaw the present-day consequences of emancipation, that the descendants of black slaves would become voting citizens and officeholders throughout the nation. But the founders left in their text no obstacles to the profound improvements that have come about. After the addition of the amendments abolishing slavery, the text retained no residue of racism, however much of it may remain in the society itself.

Therefore when the time came to terminate official segregation, we had to purge the racial provisions from federal regulations like those segregating the armed forces, and from state constitutions and state and local laws—but not from the Constitution of the United States. In fact, lawyers and judges were able to argue for profound changes by asserting that they were in accord with and demanded by the Constitution. We did not have to change it to fit new circumstances and times. Instead, the argument could be made, and was made, that conditions had to be changed to fit the Constitution. In that historic national effort, it made a very great difference that there was no racism in the original Constitution.

We must acknowledge that there was indeed intense and widespread racism among Americans, which helped to sustain for so long the vicious system of black slavery and its century-long aftermath of racial segregation, discrimination, persecution, and hatred. How best can we understand the meaning of this disjunction between the racism in the society and the absence of it in the written Constitution?

If a written constitution is not in close accord with the way the society itself is constituted, it will be irrelevant to the everyday life of the people. A constitution will be a failure if it is no more than a beautiful portrait of an ugly society. But it must be more than an accurate depiction of how the society is constituted. A good constitution provides guidance and structure for the improvement of the society. A good constitution is designed to make the political society better than it is and the citizens better persons. It must be enough like the institutions and the people to be relevant to the working of the society, but it should also have what might be called formative features, a capacity to make us better if we live according to its provisions and adhere to its institutional arrangements. The constitutional goal for Americans would be to develop a nation of self-governing, liberty-loving citizens in a new kind of political society where the fundamental rights of all would be secure—and that would mean a society where slavery would have no place.

In that formative way of thinking about the task of constitution writing, it seems entirely possible that the most foresighted and skillful of the founders sought to make a constitution that—while accepting and even protecting slavery for a time as an unavoidable evil, the price to pay for union—tried to make provisions for its ultimate extinction. They even gave thought to the constitutional preparations for a better society that would eventually be free of slavery. In that respect the original Constitution was better than the political society it constituted.

We would face a very different situation in our own time if there had been in the original Constitution any evidence of the kind of thinking ascribed to the founders by Chief Justice Taney in the *Dred Scott* case. Taney said that the founders thought that blacks were not included in the declaration that "all men are created equal," and that blacks were "so far inferior, that they had no rights which the white man was bound to respect." But Taney was wrong; there is no such racism to be found in the Constitution, then or now, not a word of it. Those who wrongly assert, however laudable their motives, that the "three-fifths clause" was racist, that it somehow denied the humanity of blacks, do a disservice to the truth and also to the Constitution, to the nation, and to the cause of justice and equality for black Americans.

Women

The fact that blacks are not mentioned in the original Constitution requires some explanation because there are several provisions obviously concerning black slavery. But no such explanation is required in the case of women. Not only are women not mentioned in the

15

original Constitution, there is no provision anywhere that applies to women as a distinct group. To the best of my knowledge, there is no evidence that the subject of women was ever mentioned in the Constitutional Convention.

This has led to the charge, heard frequently during the prolonged debate over the proposed Equal Rights Amendment, that "women were left out of the Constitution." The fact is, however, that women were not left out; they have always been included in all of the constitutional protections provided to all persons, fully and equally, without any basis in the text for discrimination on the basis of sex. How were they included without being mentioned?

The place to start is that famous provision we considered previously, Article I, section 2, clause 3, describing who will be counted for purposes of representation in the House of Representatives. The phrase "the whole number of free persons" is chiefly where the women are, but they are also among "those bound to service for a term of years," and even among taxed Indians and "all other persons." It is remarkable that they are not excluded from any one of these groups because, in 1787, women did not vote or hold office anywhere in the United States and were excluded from every level of government. What would be unremarkable, and typical of the time, would be a clear exclusion of women.

In the Northwest Ordinance, for example, we encounter provisions of this sort:

> So soon as there shall be five thousand free *male* inhabitants, of full age, in the district . . . they shall receive authority . . . to elect representatives . . . to represent them in the general assembly. . . . Provided also, that a freehold in fifty acres of land . . . shall be necessary to qualify *a man* as an elector of a representative. [Emphasis added.]

Under the terms of this famous ordinance, written in the same year as the Constitution and reaffirmed by the first Congress, which included James Madison and many other delegates to the Constitutional Convention, those who are counted for purposes of representation are men only, and voters are spoken of directly as men. That was, for the time, not at all exceptional. What is exceptional is the provision in the Constitution that everyone shall be counted. "The whole number of free persons" includes males and females. In the original Constitution, unlike the Northwest Ordinance, the words "man" or "male" do not occur, nor does any other noun or adjective denoting sex. By not mentioning women or men and speaking instead only of persons, the Constitution must mean that every right, privilege, and protection afforded to persons in the Constitution is afforded equally to female persons as well as male persons.

The terms used throughout the original Constitution are consistently what are now called nonsexist: for example, "electors," "citizens," "members," "inhabitants," "officers," "representatives," "persons." There are pronouns—"he," "his," and "himself"—but in the entire text of the original Constitution, as I have said, there is not a single noun or adjective that denotes sex.

There are some who think that because of these pronouns, all masculine, the founders meant that only men were to hold national office, and most certainly the presidency. But it can be shown that the text itself presents no obstacle whatever to having a woman in the office of president or any other national office, because these pronouns can clearly be read as generic or neutral or genderless—or whatever we call a pronoun capable of denoting either sex.

The Constitution says of the president, "*He* shall hold *his* office during the term of four years" (the emphasis here and throughout this section is added). It says that when a bill passed by Congress is presented to the president, "if *he* approves *he* shall sign it, but if not *he* shall return it," etc. There are similar usages of the pronoun for the vice president and for members of Congress. Are those pronouns exclusively masculine and therefore a definitive indication that the offices are to be held by men only, or could they be genderless pronouns, leaving open the possibility that the antecedent is meant to be either a man or a woman? If the latter is the case, as is my contention, then there is no obstacle in the Constitution, and there never has been, to a woman's occupying any office under the Constitution of the United States, including the presidency, and every protection and every right extended to men by the Constitution is extended equally to women.

My argument rests on several provisions where the masculine pronouns must certainly be read as referring to women as well as men. Consider Article IV, section 2, clause 2, providing for the return of fugitives from justice. "A person" charged with a crime who flees from justice and is found in another state shall be delivered up on demand of the governor "of the State from which *he* fled. . . ." If the "he" in this clause is assumed to mean men only, and not women, we get the absurd result that male fugitives from justice must be returned to face criminal charges, but not female fugitives.

We find similar examples in the amendments. The Fifth Amendment provides that "no person . . . shall be compelled in any criminal case to be a witness against *himself*." The Sixth Amendment provides that "in all criminal prosecutions, the accused shall enjoy the right . . .

to be confronted with the witnesses against *him;* to have compulsory process for obtaining witnesses in *his* favor, and to have the assistance of counsel for *his* defense." Will anyone seriously contend, just because the masculine pronouns are used here, that these protections were extended only to males accused in criminal prosecutions, and that the Constitution means that accused women cannot claim the same rights to confront their accusers, to compel the presence of witnesses, to be represented by a defense lawyer, and to be protected against self-incrimination?

All these examples demonstrate the absurdity of interpreting the masculine pronouns as applying to men only. And if the masculine pronouns in these provisions are genderless, then it is at least plausible that the same pronouns are genderless when used elsewhere in the same text. And if they are, and since, in fact, there is not one noun or adjective in the Constitution as ratified that in any way refers to sex, we must conclude that women are included in the Constitution, on an equal footing with men, as persons, citizens, electors, etc.—and always have been.

We are speaking, of course, of a written document, the text of the original Constitution, which is not the same as asserting that women enjoyed political equality in practice in 1787, or for a long time thereafter. Women's suffrage in the United States seems to have begun in 1838, when women in Kentucky voted in school elections. Women voted on an equal basis with men for the first time anywhere in the United States in 1869, in the Wyoming Territory. But as late as 1914, only ten more states, in addition to the state of Wyoming, had accorded women the right to vote. It was not until the Nineteenth Amendment was ratified in 1920 that the right to vote was made secure for women. That amendment provides that: "The right of citizens of the United States to vote shall not be denied or abridged by the United States or by any State on account of sex."

First we must observe that this addition to the Constitution, amended nothing and was intended to amend nothing in the Constitution of the United States. No provision in the text had to be changed or deleted, because there was never any provision in the Constitution limiting or denying the right of women to vote. The barriers to voting by women had always been in the state constitutions or laws.

It may very well be that the founders never contemplated the possibility of a woman as president, or even of women voting on an equal basis with men. Nevertheless, the text they adopted and that the American people ratified presents no obstacle whatsoever to the changes that have occurred.

Jews

The significance of not being mentioned in the Constitution becomes clearest when we consider the last of the three unmentioned subjects—Jews. Most of us, when we think of the Constitution and freedom of religion, think of the double security provided by the First Amendment, against "an establishment of religion" and for the "free exercise thereof." These protections were not, of course, part of the original Constitution. The original Constitution mentions religion just once, but that one provision is remarkable. Article VI, section 3, says simply that "no religious test shall ever be required as a qualification to any office or public trust under the United States."

Jews had suffered persecution almost everywhere in the world for millennia. Universally despised, they had been beaten, tortured, murdered, and hounded from country to country and even from continent to continent. The best they enjoyed, here and there, now and then, was a kind of safeguarded second-class status, where by one sort of decree or another they were permitted to engage in certain professions or businesses, or to live unmolested behind walls and gates in one or another section of a city. But these occasionally favorable arrangements were always precarious and often short-lived, never theirs by right but only by indulgence, not because they were entitled to decent treatment as citizens or subjects but because someone in authority had reason to protect them. Never did they have the security of political rights, not to mention the political power that comes with voting and holding office.

The question of religious tests was an old one in America and had been deliberated in every state from the moment of independence, and even before. At the time of the founding, almost every state had some form of religious test, but Jews were not the only target or even the main one. The chief concern was to bar Catholics in predominantly Protestant states, to bar some sects of Protestants in other states, and incidentally to exclude the very small numbers of "Jews, Turks, and infidels," as the saying went.

There were religious tests in the constitutions of at least eleven states, but the tests varied. Delaware required state officers to swear a Trinitarian oath; Georgia required that they be of the Protestant religion; Maryland demanded belief "in the Christian religion"—thus including Catholics as well as Protestants, but excluding Jews and nonbelievers; and New York discriminated against Catholics but did not bar Jews from holding office.[7]

Against this background we see the history-making significance of the provision prohibiting religious tests in the Constitution. Religious toleration was amazingly prevalent in America, given the intensity of religious conviction observable everywhere, but political equality for members of different religious groups was rare. That is, provisions for the free exercise of religion were common in the state constitutions; but political equality was a different story. The free exercise of religion happened in church or synagogue; it did not ensure the right to vote or hold office. Nevertheless, for whatever reasons, in a nation that had almost universal religious testing for state offices, the delegates proposed and the states ratified a constitution barring religious tests for holding national office.

Add to this the less easily discernible fact that Jews are not mentioned in the Constitution. As we view things now, that Jews are not mentioned is no more remarkable than that Baptists or Roman Catholics or Muslims or any others are also not mentioned. But Jews had never been treated simply as "persons," let alone "citizens," anywhere in the world for more than 1,500 years. By not mentioning them, that is, by not singling them out—the Constitution made Jews full citizens of a nation for the first time in all Diaspora history.[8] By this silence, coupled with the prohibition of religious tests, the founders "opened a door" to Jews and to all other sects as well.

Unspoken Principles

The Constitution of the United States is unusual, and perhaps unique, among the constitutions of the world in the way that it protects the rights of the people. The unspoken principles—at least unspoken in the Constitution—are that rights are inherent in individuals, not in the groups they belong to; that we are all equal as human beings in the sense that no matter what our color, sex, national origin, or religion, we are equal in the possession of the rights that governments are instituted to protect; and that as a consequence, the only source of legitimate political power is the consent of the governed. Because these principles, all stemming from the primacy of individual rights, are the unmentioned foundation of the Constitution, it is not only unnecessary to mention race, sex, or religion, it is inconsistent and harmful.

In short, the reason no group of any sort included in the nation it founded is mentioned in the Constitution—originally and now—is that the founders designed a better way to make sure that no one was left out, and that everyone was included on a basis of equality.

To anyone who asks why we should celebrate this Constitution, let that be the answer.

3
Of Men and Angels: A Search for Morality in the Constitution

Several cautions to the reader: Do not be misled by the theological tone of the title of this essay. Despite the reference to angels, and despite the unlikelihood that any serious political inquiry can progress very far without encountering theological questions, it is my intention to present my argument in terms wholly secular, or at least as secular as political discourse can be.

The title refers to a sentence in *The Federalist,* the great commentary on the proposed Constitution written in 1787, principally by James Madison and Alexander Hamilton, under the pen name Publius: "If men were angels, no government would be necessary." I cannot, of course, take liberties with a famous sentence from a great book, but no one should think that women are being excluded. Publius would surely have conceded the full equality of women, as I do, in this respect and in very many others, and would have agreed that women, every bit as much as men, are not angels.

Another caution: I read the sentence "If men were angels, no government would be necessary" as two linked assertions: one, that men are not angels, and, two, that government is necessary. I know, and I point out to the reader, that the sentence does not say that in so many words.

A final caution: I mean very seriously, as the subtitle indicates, that this essay is meant to be a search. What I am searching for is morality in the American Constitution. Immediately three questions present themselves:

1. Why do we have to look for it?
2. What is meant by the Constitution?
3. What morality is possible and appropriate for America?

The Two Aspects of American Morality

Why must we look for and worry about morality in the Constitution? For two good reasons. First, because so many immoral actions have besmirched our behavior in the recent past. We have had assassinations, Watergate, tawdry congressional sex scandals, corporate bribery on a worldwide scale, labor union murders, grain inspection frauds, mishandling of receipts of food stamps, cheating by medical laboratories, scandals in the management of guaranteed student loans,[1] and so on and on in a seemingly endless list that convinces many that no part of the American community is uncorrupted, that immorality is a national trait, that we are hopelessly immoral. That is one reason for searching for morality in the Constitution.

A second reason is that we are a morally judging people who make moral judgments all the time. Sometimes we judge ourselves much too high and sometimes much too low. For example, wartime rhetoric made it seem that we had no selfish national interests in the world wars and their aftermaths, that unlike every other nation, including our allies, we fought for altruistic and idealistic reasons only.

But when we are not judging ourselves too generously, we are often very severe, some would say too severe, on ourselves. During the two years of the Watergate revelations, Europeans were confused by what they called our naive reaction to government behavior that they considered just what one must expect of government officials anywhere. One intelligent and thoughtful Englishwoman told me that the American public's reaction to Watergate revelations confirmed what she had long believed about Americans, that we suffer from "moral greed." Europeans generally thought we were denigrating ourselves excessively. Even now, when the dismal facts are known, many still think so.

The fact of evildoing and the discovery of it, and our unfailing national shock, and the widespread, vehement, public condemnation that follows, are evidences of two equally significant points: that we are capable of immorality—that is, that we are not angels; and that we set very demanding moral standards of political behavior, approaching the angelic, and truly expect and demand politicians and other leaders to live up to them.

I belabor this duality because it is important for the survival of political liberty and decency in the world that we Americans have a true appraisal of ourselves. In national matters, as in personal matters, to know yourself is as important to survival as it is to happiness. And to know yourself, as we all learn from study and from experience, is one of the most difficult tasks men and women face in life. If we do not know ourselves, and hence judge ourselves by inappropriate standards, all kinds of false judgments result, too lenient or too harsh, but just right only rarely—and then only by accident.

The national danger is that by condemning ourselves or excusing ourselves unjustly—that is, by false standards—we will weaken the very forces in the world that are almost alone capable of upholding the principles of decency we love and seek to live by.

Americans are moral judgers, and severe judgers at that. More, we judge no one as severely as ourselves. This may not always have been the mass phenomenon that it is today, but elements of it have always been present in us.

That does not mean that we always, or even regularly, do the right or good thing. It means that when we do not, or when we do the wrong or evil thing, for whatever reasons of necessity, convenience, advantage, whim, passion, or ignorance, there are almost always, and almost always promptly, voices raised in self-criticism and self-condemnation. And those morally condemning voices have listeners.

Moral principle has weight and force in American political discourse. Even if we assume—as we must assume if we remember that men and women are not angels—that people act in politics primarily in pursuit of interests that are advantageous to them, and usually not advantageous or even disadvantageous to others, nevertheless, in America individuals and groups are greatly strengthened if they can connect their cause to moral principles. And if that connection is a true one, and if decent, disinterested people can see that connection readily, the case is strengthened even more, even to the extent that supporters will be enlisted whose interests might otherwise not make them allies, or might otherwise even make them opponents.

One massive example comes readily to mind, and that is the great civil rights movement of the 1950s and, especially, the 1960s. The principles of justice and equality had been available for generations to all American interest groups seeking to pursue their own advantage through political action. The fact that individual leaders like Martin Luther King and interest groups like the NAACP, CORE, and the Urban League could connect themselves, in words as well as actions, to the most powerful moral principles of the American polity multiplied their otherwise insufficient strength fivefold and more.

This combining of noble principle and self-interest, a foundation of American politics, is not hypocrisy, in my judgment. To show that black citizens gained material advantages by the legislation and court orders they obtained through moral arguments does not demean or debase the principles; it ennobles the interests. That is one way to understand Tocqueville's phrase "self-interest rightly understood"— that it is possible for selfishness to be ennobled, if not sanctified.

So seriously do Americans take morality, so politically powerful are the principles of justice and equality, that no policy, domestic or foreign, political or economic or military, can be successful, get support, be sustained, and survive setbacks that does not have a clear and acceptable moral content. It must be visible and meaningful to the Congress, the press, and above all to the American people. No matter how adroitly scheming, calculating, and self-serving individuals or groups may be, unless their suggested policies can be clothed in fitting moral garb, they will not have and hold for a sustained period the indispensable element for practical success—public support.

We can see America's moral standing more clearly in the context of a rough catalog of other nations' moral postures. For example, there are countries where a moral resignation prevails, where immoral practices are known and condoned, accepted, not resisted. There have been civil societies, of course, where morality was almost completely destroyed, so that when severe abuses of human decency occurred, the populace was not aroused in opposition and could not be aroused. There have even been societies in which almost the entire populace was eager to join in acts of cruelty and depravity.

But even in Nazi Germany, perhaps the worst example in history of an entire civilized nation corrupted and enlisted in the cause of evil, because the leaders seemed not to be sure of the thoroughness of popular commitment to evildoing, they endeavored to keep secret the mass murders in the gas ovens. And apparently they were right that many Germans, even after a decade of stern and relentless indoctrination, would have found it impossible not to condemn such immorality if it had been known to them.

Thus even when we contemplate the depths of human viciousness, there is reason to believe human nature has a strong inclination to what is morally right—something of the angel in us— and a strong aversion to what is morally wrong. There is also reason to believe that it is very difficult, but perhaps not impossible, to eliminate in almost all of us those tendencies toward what is morally right.

There are also many societies where practices that are of a lesser order of immorality, like bribery, tax evasion, nepotism, or other forms of cheating, not only occur, as they do in this country, but are accepted as part of "the way things are done." Revelations of such immoral practices do not shock the people of those countries. They simply comment, "Of course. Everybody does it."

There is probably less bribery and corruption in this country than in most others, but very far from an absence of them. In this country, however, if they are exposed, they are definitely not approved or condoned. When immoral practices are discovered and publicized,

24

the highest-ranking officials in and out of government will resign or be forced out of office. However many times examples of corruption in political or business or labor or even charitable activities are exposed, we seem never to lack the moral fervor to attack and condemn, and usually to prosecute.

I will add only one more variety of national moral posture to the brief, and surely incomplete, catalog of societies: very moral civil societies. Some such may actually have existed for a time, and some may have existed only in fiction or utopian writings; in either case, I mean civil societies where there is no corruption, no bribery, no favoritism or self-seeking, no putting self-interest ahead of the public interest—societies that might be said to be thoroughly moral in act as well as in principle.

As I understand the framers of our Constitution, on the evidence in *The Federalist* and in the debates of the Constitutional Convention, they looked at America and Americans and decided that it would be fruitless and impractical, and perhaps even morally wrong, for the new nation to strive to become spotlessly moral.

Liberty was their first principle and also their first goal. (Prosperity was their second goal.) A people that universally would put the public good ahead of private good would have to be regimented, ordered, disciplined, indoctrinated, preached to, and exhorted. Obvious institutional consequences would follow: state religion, uniform education, universal military discipline, diminution of family household influence, and curbs on commerce.

The framers knew that such a society would have to put duties first and relegate rights and everything else that is private—both low and high—to a strictly subordinate place. Self-enrichment in such a society would be scorned and replaced by concern for the moral and economic strength of the civil society as a whole. I doubt that the framers ever gave serious thought to making a nation of men and women who would be devoid of private ambition[2]—as we were told was generally the case in Mao's China, for example—but if they had given thought to it, they would have rejected it in the name of liberty and plenty.

Their own moral concern and their awareness of the character of the American people made two things clear to the framers: first, that political liberty and economic energy unavoidably engender some immorality, some cheating, and selfish advancement of private good at the expense of the public; second, that the American people are unrelenting moral judgers. The two basic American moral facts are that immorality is unavoidable and unacceptable.

25

What *Constitution* Means

The framers did not seek devices or measures to prevent all immorality, but rather to control its abuses, as consistent with the American character, consistent with the principles of liberty and equality of rights, consistent with the diversity of American ethnic origins and the multiplicity of religious sects, and consistent with the entrepreneurial energy they sought to encourage.

The reader will surely have noted that several times I have spoken of American character as the founders perceived it, as if the nation had already been formed before its founding. To a large extent I think that was the case. Consider a little simple arithmetic. If we take 1619, the date of the establishment of the Virginia House of Burgesses, the first American legislative body, as a starting point, it was 170 years later that the Constitution was ratified. That means that it was not until 1959, during the lifetime of most of those old enough to be concerned about morality in politics, that Americans had as long a political experience on this continent since the Constitution as before it. If you have a feeling for how long ago 1789 was, you can feel how long a time the American people had to develop a character of their own before the written Constitution.

That character derived from many factors, including religion (most of the sects were dissenters); experience in self-government (the legislatures of many colonies had considerable power, including power of the purse); political doctrines emphasizing liberty and equality (from John Locke preeminently); and unusual, even unprecedented economic conditions.

Consider the economic conditions for a moment. Adam Smith describes tellingly in *The Wealth of Nations,* published in 1776, the consequences of placing cultured Europeans, especially cultured in agriculture, on a vast and fertile continent, almost uninhabited and pretty much free for the taking. His chapter "Causes of the Prosperity of New Colonies" begins thus: "The colony of a civilized nation which takes possession either of a waste country, or one so thinly inhabited, that the natives easily give place to the new settlers, advances more rapidly to wealth and greatness than any other human society." In seventeenth- and eighteenth-century America, labor was in short supply relative to demand. Wages were high, and conditions were favorable to the worker. It was hard to hold on to hired hands because it was so easy for them to save enough in a short time to move off to start their own enterprise, usually farming their own piece of land, and there was plenty of open space to move on to.

The situation was favorable for the flowering of respect for the free individual's rights, because those who were not slaves had to be treated well to keep them on the job, since they had so many opportunities everywhere. Where every hand is valuable, if you can't enslave him or her, you have to pay a high price for that person's labor. And what you pay dearly for, you value highly. But even if an employer did treat employees or indentured servants well, he was likely to lose them in a fairly short time, a few years usually, because it was so easy for newcomers with ambition to strike out on their own. In such circumstances, where the demand for labor exceeds the supply, slavery is also very attractive. If you can assure yourself of a large enough number of laborers and any way of keeping them, where naturally rich unowned land is abundant, your profit is ensured. Slavery and the principles of liberty and equality that ultimately led to its destruction grew out of the same soil.

The combination of propitious economic, political, and religious factors contributed to the development of tastes, inclinations, habits, and institutions among Americans that were strong and deeply ingrained when the Constitution was written in 1787. The relevance of the pre-existing American character, in my understanding of it, can be explained by the simple device of sometimes writing the word *constitution* with a capital *C*, to denote that I mean the frame of government, in our case set forth in a written document, and sometimes writing it with a small *c*, to denote that I mean something different, which I will now try to explain.

If we speak of the American constitution- with a small *c*—we could mean the way Americans are constituted: their character, their habits, their manners, their morals, their tastes, their countryside, their strengths, their weaknesses, their speech, their songs, their poems, their books, their sports, their machines, their arts, their heroes, their dress, their ceremonies, their homes and families, and their ways of conducting business. All of this, and more, would tell us how Americans *are constituted*. And since much of what is included in such a list would be the result of conscious effort and decision, it would also be possible to speak of how Americans *have constituted themselves*. Thus, considering how long Americans were on this continent before 1787, it is perfectly intelligible to speak of what the American constitution was before the Constitution of the United States was written, as well as to speak of the formative influence the Constitution of the United States had, subsequently, on the American constitution.

The document called the Constitution names itself in the Preamble as "this Constitution for the United States of America," but it could just as well have been called "the Articles," or "the Charter," or "the Covenant," or "the Compact," or "the Polity," or a number of other suitable names. When the Congress sent it to the original thirteen states for ratification, they gave it no caption. In most states, when it was printed for the use of the delegates of ratifying conventions and for public information, it was entitled "A Frame of Government."

The word *constitution* for this purpose grew in usage in the century from 1689 to 1789, from the Glorious Revolution to the adoption of the Constitution. Before that, the usage pointed more to the way things were ordered. According to the Oxford English Dictionary, *constitution* meant "the way in which anything is constituted or made up; the arrangement or combination of its parts or elements, as determining its nature and character. E.g., constitution of nature, of the world, of the universe, etc." The political usage indicated "the mode in which a state is constituted or organized, especially as to the location of the sovereign power, as a monarchical, oligarchical, or democratic constitution."

But *Constitution* grew out of this usage as a fitting word for a document that seeks to apply an appropriate frame of government to a people who are constituted in a discernible way. A well-designed Constitution records and proclaims how we are constituted and how we intend to be constituted for the future. Whether the Constitution is written or not, every political community has a constitution, because to be a political community it must have an accepted ordering of things and a location of the sovereign power.

Let the exception prove the rule. When we ask whether a nation ruled by a dictatorial individual or group has a Constitution, we are stretching the concept to its breaking point. For example, some nations are described as constitutional monarchies, signifying that some other monarchies are not constitutional. What we mean is that absolute monarchies have no discernible order in the ruling, that the monarch can act without restraint, without law, according to whim, not only with unlimited powers, but arbitrarily. That is why John Locke said that "absolute monarchy . . . can be no form of civil government at all."[3] And I say that any nation has a constitution, but at times there may be no Constitution and its unconstitutional rulers may not be a government.

When nations that have been ruled by tyrants overthrow them and form a new and constitutional government, they demonstrate that they had a constitution all along; that is that they were constituted a certain way and are now able to frame a government that is thought to suit the way they are constituted. And that frame of government may properly be called the Constitution. It is in this sense that we say that nations get the government they deserve.

My thesis is that the framers considered the constitution of the American people—what they were and what they were capable of being and doing—and drew up the Constitution of the United States. They did not want to leave Americans just where they were; instead starting where they were, they wanted to make them better. As was once written, long ago, by a non-American: "Lawgivers make the citizens good by training them in habits of right action—that is the aim of all lawmaking, and if it fails to do this it is a failure; this is what distinguishes a good Constitution from a bad one."[4]

The framers did not seek to remake Americans, but rather to take them as they were and lead them to habits of right action. Their task was to direct the powerful American tendency to self-interest and self-advancement so that abuses would be controlled. More, they aimed not only to control these tendencies but actually to turn them to the benefit of the people.

Other societies have tried to curb or eliminate selfish ambition and selfish interest out of a reasonable fear that when those inclinations are combined with political power, tyranny often results and the people often lose their freedom. The constitutional scheme in other societies has relied on measures such as rigorous education in the virtues of selflessness, or constant surveillance, strict discipline, and severe punishment.

The American constitutional scheme is explained briefly in *The Federalist*. Put separate parts of political power in the hands of different officials in different parts of the government—legislative, executive, and judicial—and encourage, if they need encouragement, ambition and self-interest. "Ambition must be made to counteract ambition," Publius says. "The interest of the man must be connected with the constitutional rights of the place."[5] By this means, the abuses of power by one official, or several, will be opposed by others who have strong and natural incentives that need no inculcation or exhortation. In fact, if officials in one part of the government should be insufficiently moved by ambition and self-interest, a necessary balancing restraint would be lacking, and the danger of concentration of power in the hands of others would increase. It seems that there is a need for very many ambitious and self-interested officials to keep our government in balance. As fundamental as separation of powers is as a principle of the Constitution, even more fundamental is the need for officeholders to be ambitious and self-interested.

Are these the habits of right action the Constitution aims to train us in? In part, the answer is yes. In part, however, the answer must also be that the Constitution seeks to train us in habits of restraint and moderation, because that is the only way ambitious officeholders can contend with other ambitious officeholders without falling victim to the law or to power struggles.

It is a system for nonangels who nevertheless are convinced that men and women are good enough to govern themselves. What is clear is that it is a frame of government for a people so constituted that clashing with each other almost without cease is the expected daily routine.

In a discourse on the work of Isaac Newton, Thomas Simpson of St. John's College in Santa Fe made this comparison:

> Our Republic was designed in the image of Isaac Newton's vision of the System of the World, set forth in the Third Book of his *Principia*. Hobbes had taught man to regard the state as an artifice to rescue himself from war and his own nature, but it was Newton who showed how exactly-counter-working forces could be composed to form a harmonious and lasting system—and this composition of forces in the system of planets about the sun was the ultimate paradigm for the authors of our Constitution as they attempted to solve the three-body problem of the legislative, the executive, and the judicial powers.
>
> Newton, then, showed how the cosmos might be grasped by the mind as a purposeful system, an intelligent design; the authors of our Constitution showed the world in turn how man could make this insight, out of mathematical physics, serve him in the design of a balanced and rational polity.[6]

I would not dare to quarrel with Dr. Simpson about Newton, but would only accept his guidance respectfully and gratefully and do my best to understand. But the notion of the Constitution of the United States as "harmonious" is very wide of the mark. Much closer, I think, is the description of Tocqueville in capturing the character of the American constitution and political system: "No sooner do you set foot on American soil than you find yourself in a sort of tumult; a confused clamor rises on every side, and a thousand voices are heard at once, each expressing some social requirements."[7] Tumult, confused clamor, a thousand voices—not harmony—that is how America was and is constituted.[8] And the framers wisely chose, I think, not to strive to change it, but rather to institutionalize it.

If that is the American constitution, the morality most characteristic of America, then and now, is what might be called a measured, a restrained, a moderated, or even a mean morality. It does not ignore or condone immorality. In fact, it holds morality very high in public esteem. As I have argued, no public policy can gain and hold the support of the American people if its moral content is not laudable and apparent to the people generally. A policy may be begun, it may be continued for a time, but if it lacks moral acceptability it cannot be sustained. But the morality that is needed must commence with the understanding that men and women are not angels.

Moderate Morality

Awareness that we are not angels has complex significance. It does not mean that we are evil or unrelievedly selfish. It does mean that we acknowledge that our basic motivation is self-interest and that there is a need to control the unavoidable abuses that follow from that self-ishness. From somewhere, perhaps out of our selfishness—that is, out of the sense of justice that derives from the sense of injustice (which is easily come by from the natural dislike of acts of unfairness to ourselves)—there comes a strong sense of morality, of fairness, or aversion to unfairness. And this strong sense of morality leads frequently to an excess of morality. Men and women sometimes indulge themselves in excesses of morality, and such self-indulgence and excess have the same distorting effects as do all other forms of extremism. Measure or restraint or moderation is not misplaced in matters of morality.

The morality most appropriate to the American way, to the American constitution as it was even before the founding and as it still is, is a morality that is moderate, that does not crusade, that accepts the fact that among human beings who are free there will be abuses, and that does not seek to eradicate all evil from the face of the earth, knowing that such moral attempts are excessive and often lead to monstrous immorality. Though we sometimes use the rhetoric, we are not true to ourselves and to our national character when we crusade, domestically or in foreign policy.

Consider the story of Carmen. When her soldier-lover hears the bugle call summoning him back to camp, she warns him that if he goes she will not meet him again. He explains that the regulations require him to report at an appointed hour, and Carmen replies with the famous line, "Gypsy love knows no law." So it is with unbounded moralism. Alluring and seductive, it too knows no law. The morality of our constitution is very much a bounded and law-abiding morality.

When I speak of the American character and its morality, I do not mean that we are consistent in our tendencies and reactions. Thank goodness that we are not, and that life is not so simple and dull. The truth is, and all of us know it, that as a nation we have a multiplicity of reactions, a multiplicity of individuals and groups tending to go in a multiplicity of directions; and sometimes, a multiplicity of tendencies contend within each of us.

One of these common tendencies is for us to shrug our shoulders when we hear one more revelation of wrongdoing. It does get tiresome, after all. We develop an aversion less to the wrongdoer and more to the moralizers and wish they would do us all a favor and just shut up.

At other times we become mightily aroused; we judge quickly and harshly; we preach to others and volunteer our services as policemen to the world, ready, like Superman, to fly anywhere in the world to fight evil, at whatever cost of pain and treasure.

Sometimes, however—and at these times we are at our best, in my estimation, and most true to our real constitution—we judge and act with measured restraint, with moderation. We do not ignore the presence of evil, nor do we try to exterminate it and, perhaps, many valuable things with it. The Constitution is designed to help foster this restraint.

Practical or political morality always involves two related but separable and distinct steps. The first step, and an essential one for a moral person, is to face the fact of wrongdoing and judge it. When we fail to take that step, we slip into our worst amoral lethargy; fortunately for us as a nation that strives for decency, failure to make a moral judgment happens rarely, and when it happens it is possible for us to be roused from it, for we are not deaf to moral suasion. So the first step is to make the moral judgment, to recognize evil as evil and not look the other way or refuse to judge (on relativistic grounds) or shrug our shoulders and say we don't care.

But making a moral judgment does not settle the question of policy. The second step remains: to ask ourselves, what shall we do about it? There are moral as well as practical considerations involved in the second step. The first-step moral judgment may tell us that something ought to be done, but it leaves to deliberation what that something might be.

The best example of this I know in American history is the consistent position of Abraham Lincoln on the question of slavery. The first step was easy for him, and he made it clearly and persistently in all of his public utterances, notably in his debates with Stephen Douglas. On the question of the extension of slavery into new states and territories not yet slave territory, Douglas said "I don't care" whether it is voted up or voted down. Let the local people on the spot decide for themselves—local rule, self-determination.

Lincoln said in response what must be said first: that slavery was wrong and that we cannot say "I don't care" whether this immoral institution is extended and strengthened. After all, he argued, we are the children of the Declaration of Independence, and there are principles that will not let us alone, that we cannot turn our backs on and still remain Americans. That was the first step.

As for the second step, Lincoln said he was not an abolitionist, just as he would not be a slaveholder. Abolitionists looked on the Constitution as an abomination, a compact with the Devil, and they regularly burned a copy of the Constitution at their meetings. That is an example of the unbounded moralism I spoke of, which in its crusading striking out at evil is likely to destroy with it many good things—the Constitution, in this case—that give us, ultimately, our best hope for preserving decency in political life. Lincoln, unlike the abolitionists, sought a way to end slavery without destroying the Union and the Constitution, the instrumentalities of our liberties.

Thus even after the Civil War had commenced, Lincoln was still trying to develop and get acceptance for a plan of gradual and compensated emancipation of the slaves. His plan could have taken as long as thirty-five years to complete, and no force would have been used. During that time there would be no spread of slavery, and the more it was diminished by purchase of the freedom of slaves from slaveholders, the weaker would become the proslavery forces.

Many would condemn a policy that would prolong enslavement for some for decades and pay slaveholders for slaves they had no moral right to own. But Lincoln thought that Americans, North and South, shared the blame for slavery and that the chief task was less to punish wrongdoers than to right the wrong. He thought some slavery could be tolerated so long as its increase was halted, its diminution ensured, and its termination achieved without massive bloodshed, without confiscating what some people claimed under the law was property, without disrupting the Union, and without weakening or possibly destroying the Constitution.

Lincoln's plan for gradual compensated emancipation was not so much rejected as ignored. Instead, the Civil War went on; the matter was settled by unbounded moralists on both sides of the controversy; and as a result we had horrendous warfare, a divided nation, and deep-seated bitterness that has not fully abated more than a century later.

In the light of all I have now said about how I think the founders, or Publius, thought about this question and what the consequences are of the fact that men and women are not angelic, consider the brief passage that is the basis for what I have said, and judge my interpreta-

self: "Ambition must be made to counteract ambition. of the man must be connected with the constitutional place. It may be a reflection on human nature, that such d be necessary to control the abuses of government. But nment itself but the greatest of all reflections on human nature? If men were angels, no government would be necessary."

Self-Righteousness and Righteousness

If I am right about what kind of political morality is truly American, about what kind of morality truly fits the way we have constituted ourselves as a nation, there remains still a problem of grave proportions: the question of attractiveness.

In a democratic republic such as ours, where public opinion and popular taste rule, ultimately, on everything, measures and policies must be attractive to hundreds of millions of people to gain the support that is essential to sustain them.

There is something drab and unsatisfying in moral moderation. There is a natural yearning for something higher and purer. All that aiming lower has to recommend it is that it works, but that leaves many of the best of men and women restless and dissatisfied. The search for excitement and inspiration in moderation is fruitless. For example, the only conclusion one can come to after reading the famous essay by William James, "The Moral Equivalent of War," is that there is no moral equivalent of war.

Between extremes lies a mean; it is worth pointing out that the word *mean* is, at the very least, ambiguous. One can try to dress it in finery and speak of the golden mean, but there just is no glitter in mean morality. Moderation or measure or restraint or seeking the mean in anything is not the kind of cause for which people devise banners and slogans. It is hard to compose a marching song or an inspirational poem in praise of sobriety or moderation. You cannot have neon borders flashing on and off, and brass bands parading, and cheering sections screaming at the top of their voices if the message is: "Be moderate." You can't even write such a command with an exclamation point without turning it into a joke.

Some words are suited for whispers or a soft voice: "Kiss me" or "I love you." Others can be shouted or screamed: "Hit him!" or "Kill the umpire!" or "Stop thief!" But moderation can be neither whispered nor shouted. To whisper "moderation" is insipid, and to shout it is ridiculous. Moderation is truly a mean word.

And yet unless this notion of moderation, of bounded morality, is widely accepted, it will be hard for us to think of ourselves as a truly moral nation, for that is the morality that fits us. And that conviction,

34

that we are truly a moral nation of moral men and moral women, is essential to our survival and happiness, because of the way we are constituted. We need to believe it; and for us to believe it, it must be true. We have for a long time been the world's best hope that political decency might prevail widely. There are still, out there in the rest of the world, billions of persons longing to be free. A vitalized America, confident of its own strength and its own rectitude, is their best hope that things might ever change for the better. A sense of our own rectitude is our Samson's long hair; without it we have no strength. That is what enables us to say that "right makes might," which is not to say that right *is* might.

What is the chief obstacle to sustaining our confidence in our national rectitude? In large part it is our powerful sense of morality and our aversion to hypocrisy. Our strong moral sense judges and condemns our weaker moral practice. Being strongly moral, we declare ourselves immoral. The judge, out of an abundance of morality, declares the culprit immoral, but the judge and the culprit are one and the same. Is there any solution, any way for the judge to see himself as a constant moral judge as well as an inconstant immoral culprit and—on the whole—a righteous people?

I think so, and I think Publius has shown us the way. It rests on the difference between righteousness and self-righteousness. What is that difference? If we can answer that question, we can chart a course to the national self-confidence we need, for our own sake, for the sake of political decency, and for the sake of the hopes of oppressed men and women everywhere.

Because men and women are not angels, the standard of human righteousness cannot be that one act as an angel would. The standard must be something akin to our humanity, to our nonangelic state of being. For us nonangels, a righteous person is one who strives to live and act by the light of righteous principles, which include, surely, respect for the equal rights of others to life, liberty, property, and the pursuit of happiness. Trying to follow the guidance of America's standard political principles is the first element of human-scale political righteousness, whether one always succeeds or not.

We would have to add, of course, that trying is not enough in itself; there must be a fairly high degree of success. But above all there must be a recognition that because we are not angels, and because we have freedom, there will be failures, there will be fallings off, there will be abuses, and that there must be "devices" for controlling and dealing with these failures. The devices—including ambition counteracting ambition—must be bounded, and legal, and habitual, and even institutional. If we describe a people such as that—guided by right principles, usually living in accord with them, sometimes failing

35

to measure up, rarely in doubt about what the standards ought to be, seeking to punish abuses and prevent them but too committed to liberty to seek to root out all the possible causes of future human failings—we are describing a nonangelic, but decidedly righteous, people.

Now what about self-righteousness? Self-righteousness is rightly scorned. Self-righteousness is an excess of righteousness, a distortion and disfigurement of righteousness; it is righteousness without moderation. It is more easily recognized in the flesh than defined in words. Self-righteousness is not only boring but hateful; it has been the soruce of many of the most vicious and inhuman acts in the annals of history, and on a grand scale.

The self-righteous person mistakes the rectitude of his principles for his own rectitude. He confounds his beliefs and his behavior. In his mind he converts his professed righteous principles into a person, and thinks he is that person. Righteousness and "self" become as one. This confusion enables him, in the name of the highest principles of morality, to consider himself the appointed enforcer of morality, the embodiment of righteousness, as if he were the Avenging Angel, or any angel rather than a human being.

Publius is our guide in thus singling out and condemning the self-righteous moralist. In the simplest terms, the self-righteous person forgets the difference between human beings and angels. Self-righteousness in personal matters is distressing enough, but in government it is especially ludicrous, for "if men were angels, no government would be necessary."

The search for morality leads us to the necessity for another quest. We must find the ways—not through showmanship but through reasoning, which in most times and places has been attractive to young and other sound minds—to appeal to the best in us and to persuade us that we have and always have had what is needed to be a righteous people. Nothing that has happened since we started to constitute ourselves as one people more than three hundred and fifty years ago, and nothing that has happened since we declared our founding principles and wrote down our Constitution more than two hundred years ago, has diminished the possibilities of righteousness and morality on a national scale, so long as we do not confuse righteousness and self-righteousness.

The key to our political salvation, if such combining of the secular and the divine may be allowed, is the lesson inherent in the most basic principle of the American constitution: Men and women are not angels.

4
How the Constitution Promotes Progress

The Constitution of the United States was the world's first written national constitution. In 1787 it was the only one; now approximately 160 nations have written constitutions. No other nation's constitution has come close to ours in longevity. In fact, the constitutions of other nations are usually so short-lived, they need to be replaced so often, that it is becoming rare for one to survive for a few decades, let alone centuries.

More than half of the written national constitutions in effect today throughout the world have been adopted since 1974. This means that new national constitutions have been coming into existence at a rate of more than five every year. These new constitutions are being written not only by relatively new nations like Nigeria and Zimbabwe, but also by old ones like Spain, Portugal, Greece, Turkey, and Canada. And so, in the year that we celebrated the two hundredth anniversary of the Constitution of the United States, the median age of all other written constitutions in the world was about thirteen years.

What accounts for the remarkable stability and longevity of our Constitution? That is a question I have been asked repeatedly by constitutional experts in other countries, and of course there is no certain answer. Some of it surely must be ascribed to good luck, that is, to factors not entirely of our own doing, for which we Americans cannot claim credit. Further, we must always remember that the Constitution originally had a very serious defect, which divided the nation irreconcilably and nearly brought the Constitution and the Union to an inglorious end. We had to fight a bloody Civil War because the problems of slavery could not be resolved by political and constitutional processes. In the end, however, the Constitution was not only preserved, it was strengthened by the established constitutional amending procedure.

But having acknowledged its imperfections, we must also acknowledge that its durability is probably best ascribed to its unusual excellences. It has lasted so long because it commands the respect and loyalty and affection of the people. Consider its main features:

• It establishes *limited government*, based on the principle that, because all human beings have inherent personal rights, some things are just none of the government's business. As a result, Americans have always enjoyed an unusual measure of personal and political freedom.

• It provides a system of *separation of powers*, with built-in checks and balances, which prevents excesses of power most of the time, and detects and reliably punishes, at other times, such excesses as do occur.

• It builds a *federal* structure, which helps to ensure widespread citizen participation in local self-government throughout an extended national territory.

• It secures *freedoms* of speech, press, and religion, matters that we consider natural, right, and commonplace, but that are rare in most other parts of the world.

• And it provides in an unusual manner the essential conditions for *economic growth*. This last requires further explanation.

In 1787, the American nation was just beginning to understand the processes of economic growth. There were at that time still persisting remnants of mercantilism, with its preference for government regulation, and of feudalism, with its preference for property in land over commercial property.

Although we see in the text of the Constitution no evidence of feudal or mercantilist thought, we also see almost no clues to economic doctrines of any other sort. The framers did not spell out an economic system, as is now commonly done in the constitutions of many other nations. There are instead a number of somewhat scattered clauses, such as that states cannot adopt laws that impair the obligation of contracts, and that the Congress shall have power to levy taxes, borrow money, coin money and fix its value, make uniform bankruptcy laws, regulate commerce with foreign nations, and so on.

One clause, however, does give a strong indication of the economic thinking of the framers. The first article of the Constitution establishes the legislative branch of the new government and enumerates the powers it shall have. Among these new powers—such as to make uniform rules for naturalization, to establish post offices, to constitute the federal courts, to raise armies and maintain a navy, and so on—we find an unusual one that begins as follows:

The Congress shall have power to promote the progress of science and useful arts, by. . . .

That is the way the clause begins, but I have left it unfinished, for the moment, to allow us to consider how best one might complete it. Imagine yourself a delegate to the convention and that it has just been decided that Congress should have such a power. How should a constitution-writer complete the sentence, in twenty words or less, to state how Congress is to go about this new task of promoting progress?

The possibilities are numerous. Congress could establish a nationwide educational system. It could establish a national university with admission on a strict competitive basis. It could establish specialized national research institutes or award prizes for the best research papers, inventions, and literary works. Congress could establish an agency for national testing to find the most promising youngsters for special instruction and support.

None of these is a bad idea, and all have been adopted, in the United States or elsewhere, in one form or another, over the years. More to the point, none of these would have been a new or strange idea to the delegates to the convention, for all of them had already been tried or advocated in one place or another.

All the more striking then is the way in which our constitution writers did choose to complete the sentence. The completed clause reads as follows:

> The Congress shall have power to promote the progress of science and useful arts, by securing for limited times to authors and inventors the exclusive right to their respective writings and discoveries.

In short, of all the ways the convention delegates might have chosen, the one they decided on was to secure by legislation the possibility of profiting in the marketplace. (There is one other remarkable feature of this clause, this is the only place in the original Constitution where the word *right* occurs.)

How did they come to this formulation? We can only speculate on the answer to that question because there is no record of any discussion of this provision in the constitutional convention. But the delegates were men of ideas, leaders and innovators themselves. Among them was Benjamin Franklin, considered by contemporaries around the world to be one of the most inventive practical thinkers of his time. These men knew, at least as well as any similar group would know today, that the desire for profit, no matter how powerful it might be in other respects, cannot make a man or woman thoughtful or inventive, and that the promise of money cannot by itself produce new ideas.

39

We know and they knew that it is foolish to think that the best writers, artists, researchers, and inventors care so much about money that they would not experiment or compose music or paint or write plays or inquire unless there were a profit. I mean more than to evoke the romantic fictional image of the starving poet in an unheated garret. We have enough real examples of great minds and ultimate benefactors of mankind who went unrecognized and unrewarded all of their lives yet never ceased their productive work. Only one who is ignorant of the true nature of innovative effort could think that without the profit motive no useful contributions would be made to human progress.

What then was in the minds of the constitution-writers? The best brief explanation I know was provided many decades later in one sentence by Abraham Lincoln, who said of this constitutional provision that it "added the fuel of interest to the fire of genius, in the discovery and production of new and useful things."

Lincoln made a helpful distinction. Genius has its own fire. The desire to decipher the mysteries of nature and of nature's laws, to make something that has never before existed, to say what has never before been said—these have a compelling power of their own. The love of wisdom or knowledge or understanding is, in a significant way, nonpolitical, nonsocietal. Its motivation is internal. It cannot be originated by constitutional provisions, no matter how skillfully drawn and implemented. But it can be fueled—encouraged, nurtured, protected, rewarded, and thus enhanced.

Genius, the power and originality of mind that produces new thought, new understanding, new inventions, has its own "fire" that society at-large cannot plan, schedule, or produce. It ignites, happily, in unpredictable persons, times, and places, and when it does it is an individual and private matter.

But societies need such innovative genius; they neglect it at the risk of their own impoverishment. What the framers understood, and what Lincoln's sentence illuminates so well, is that the best that society at-large can do is provide more fuel for the fire of genius. That fuel, as we know, can come in various forms—well-equipped laboratories, research assistance, a collegial setting with competent colleagues, opportunities for study, time for reflection and writing, prizes and honors, and the monetary rewards associated with copyrights and patents.

The constitutional provision we have been considering is commonly called, of course, the "copyright and patent clause," despite the fact that those two words do not occur anywhere in the Constitution. But it seems to me a great pity that it is not known as the "progress clause," to focus our thinking on how the authors of the Constitution meant the government and the private sector to be related and how they hoped the nation would progress. They assumed that people work better when they have a material incentive, that it is unjust for an inventor to have no special advantage from his own invention, and that society has a stake in seeing that those who make contributions that the rest of us need are kept happily productive by being rewarded.

Innovative work can be rewarded in many ways. Even a state-controlled economy provides many forms of reward for accomplishment considered unusually valuable to the state—promotion, high salaries, honorific titles, a deluxe apartment, a country home, servants, medals, a limousine with driver, and so on. These rewards may not seem very different from those that success brings in our own system, but there is one major difference: they are all in the power of the government or party officials to bestow or withhold, and this influences and often dictates the kind of work undertaken and rewarded.

Under a proper reading of the "progress clause," the decisions about which research questions to ask, what experiments to conduct, what products to design and produce, which books to write, are all left to private persons. The system of reward is determined by the preferences and decisions of countless individuals in the private sector, forces that are difficult or impossible for free governments to control.

What then have we learned about the way the founders intended to provide for economic growth? The clues in this "progress clause" suggest that they saw progress as a national concern, but springing from private endeavor and enterprise, that government does not have the primary role, that monopoly should be avoided (exclusive right *for limited times*) in favor of competition, and that the prospect of profit should be recognized and approved as a powerful incentive for private effort and public progress.

Of all the forms of encouragement and reward one can think of "to promote the progress of science and useful arts," the one most appropriate to a free society and therefore the one most appropriate in a constitution devoted to securing the individual rights of the people is just the one the founders chose.

5

What Americans Know about
Their Constitution

"Americans today have a confused understanding of many of the Constitution's basic tenets and provisions" and "a poor grasp of some elemental American history." This was the finding of a national survey conducted by Research & Forecasts and sponsored by the Hearst Corporation in late 1986. Entitled "The American Public's Knowledge of the U.S. Constitution," the survey led its analysts to conclude that American ignorance of the Constitution is "a problem in need of a remedy."

These poll results were reported widely and with considerable editorial dismay. Apparently considered most alarming was that 45 percent of the American public think that the Constitution includes the phrase "From each according to his ability, to each according to his need," the egalitarian Marxist formulation directly opposed to the idea of monetary incentives. Other examples: only 34 percent know approximately how many constitutional amendments there are; 64 percent think the Constitution establishes English as the national language; only 41 percent identify the Bill of Rights as the first ten amendments to the original Constitution; 60 percent "incorrectly say the president, acting alone, can appoint a justice to the Supreme Court"; and only 43 percent know that William Rehnquist is the chief justice.

These answers confirmed what most of us might have guessed without a national survey—if we give adult Americans a high school–style quiz on the text of the Constitution or on dates and facts of any other aspect of American history, they will not score well.

During the past few years I have been conducting my own informal, unscientific survey on knowledge of the text of the Constitution. When I speak to a college audience—students, faculty, and general public—about the Constitution, I ask how many think they know the five opening words of the Bill of Rights ("Congress shall make no law . . ."). In audiences of hundreds rarely are as many as ten hands raised; and of those who think they know, usually more than half have the wrong answer.

Their ignorance of the text of the First Amendment, however, is balanced by strong evidence that college students know full well that freedom of speech is one of their constitutional rights. They exercise it energetically, whether or not they know the text.

Ignorance of the words of the great document revealed by the Hearst survey is disappointing, of course, and one can well understand the concern expressed in editorials and in public statements. As one example, former Chief Justice Warren Burger has in speech after speech cited this survey as further evidence of the need for public education about the Constitution.

A Confused Public?

The effectiveness of the Constitution depends to a large extent on the public's support of it, and that support derives from our understanding of it. But does this survey show that the Constitution is in danger because we misunderstand the document? How alarmed should we be? That depends on how well the survey measures our understanding of the Constitution.

The Hearst poll reports that "nearly half (45 percent) say the Marxist declaration 'From each according to his ability, to each according to his need' is found in the Constitution." Can it be that Americans are unable to distinguish American constitutionalism from Marxism? Let's take a closer look.

The respondents were answering a question that was posed as a combination of true/false and multiple choice, in this fashion: "True or false: The following phrases are found in the U.S. Constitution." There followed five phrases, three from the Declaration of Independence, one from the Gettysburg Address, and one from Karl Marx. None of the phrases offered was from the Constitution. The correct answer to all five phrases was "false."

But respondents, reacting as they might to an American history high school quiz, apparently were looking for "the right answer." They went strongly for "Of the people, by the people, for the people" (82 percent); "All men are created equal" (80 percent); "Life, liberty, and the pursuit of happiness" (77 percent); and "The consent of the governed" (52 percent). Marx came in last, well behind Abraham Lincoln and Thomas Jefferson.

How many of the 45 percent who answered "true" to "From each according to his ability . . ." would have volunteered that phrase as part of the Constitution without prompting? We have no way to be certain from what the survey tells us, but my guess is, not one in thousands.

As for what the survey report calls the American public's "confusion" of the Declaration of Independence with the Constitution, it seems to me not at all a bad thing that Americans associate our Constitution with phrases such as "consent of the governed" and "all men are created equal." They might be "the wrong answers" on a quiz, but as a citizen's view of our governing principles, it seems to me all to the good.

In fact, there are serious constitutional scholars who argue, as I do, that the principles of the Declaration are embedded (without being mentioned explicitly) in the Constitution. The rights we enjoy under the Constitution are individual rights, ours because we are human beings, not because we belong to any particular group. There is no mention in the original Constitution of any group identified by race, color, religion, nationality, sex, or language. Because the rights of all are protected as "persons" or "citizens" without any other identification, the message is that no one is left out, that we are all included on the basis of equality. (The proof of this principle is best seen in the only exception. Indians *are* mentioned for the purpose of *excluding* them.)

For anyone who has trouble accepting that there are principles included in the Constitution that are not mentioned, consider this partial list: federalism, separation of powers, judicial review, separation of church and state, and checks and balances. All of these are certainly "embedded" in the Constitution; none of them is mentioned.

So one should be very hesitant to say that it is "incorrect" to think that some principle is not really part of the Constitution just because it is not stated explicitly in the text. They may not always have the texts straight, but I do not see the evidence in this survey that the American public is confused about how much of the Declaration of Independence is in the Constitution.

Principled Ignorance

Only if you think of the Constitution as a homework assignment to quiz kids on the next day would you design a survey as Hearst did. If, instead, you think of the Constitution more broadly, as the framework of government that guides and shapes our national life, you will not judge the American people as confused because they think the

Constitution includes the phrases "of the people, by the people, for the people," and "all men are created equal."

In sum, I do not share the alarm of the Hearst Corporation about the American public's "ignorance" of the Constitution. Their answers, even when wrong on a strictly textual basis, are far from being incorrect. Americans may not have the text of the Constitution in their heads, but they have the meaning of it in their hearts and in their bones.

If we grade the American public C-minus for their answers, what grade shall we give to Frank A. Bennack, Jr., president and chief executive officer of the Hearst Corporation? In his preface to the report, Mr. Bennack began with this historical howler:

> On September 17, 1787, the twelfth year of our nation's independence, a group of some of the most venerable figures in American history signed their names to a document which was to become the charter for the first successful experiment in self-government in the modern era.
> One of those venerable gentlemen, Thomas Jefferson . . .

The fact is that Thomas Jefferson was not there. While the framers were in Philadelphia writing the Constitution, Jefferson was in Paris serving as the American minister to France. He had no part in the signing of the Constitution. Anyone can confirm this by checking the signatures that *are* part of the text of the Constitution.

I conclude that if 100 percent of Hearst Corporation chief executive officers incorrectly volunteer the name of Thomas Jefferson, without prompting, as a signer of the Constitution, then the American people score somewhat better than those who design surveys to test them. But Bennack's obvious understanding of and commitment to the great principles of the Constitution only confirm what I have said about the Hearst survey: some ignorance of the text of the Constitution can be compatible with a sound understanding of it and a deep and loving dedication to its tenets. Jefferson's principles are embedded in the Constitution despite his absence from the signing.

The Hearst report serves us well by showing the public's ignorance of some very important provisions of the Constitution. My criticism is that its authors thought that ignorance of the text also indicated misunderstanding of the constitutional principles. Instead, the "incorrect" answers show that Americans have a pretty good sense of the essential spirit of the Constitution. But, yes, it would be better if more of us also knew the words.

6

Is There an American Right of Revolution?

If the most widely read and widely approved American book on the Declaration of Independence were right, twentieth-century Americans would be wrong to continue to cherish the Declaration as a national treasure. Carl Becker, the late, eminent Cornell University historian, in his book *The Declaration of Independence*, argued that the famous second paragraph of the Declaration is "a frank assertion of the right of revolution," which is useful doctrine when revolution is wanted but a nuisance when stability and preservation of the status quo are sought. Becker concluded that the Declaration of Independence and "the right of revolution" began to lose their relevance for the United States soon after the Constitution was adopted and went out of vogue in America, completely and permanently, early in the nineteenth century.

The Right of Revolution

I think that Becker was wrong; the Declaration of Independence does not assert the right of revolution. That phrase, by the way, ascribed by many, Becker among them, to John Locke, does not occur in Locke's writings, nor does it occur in the Declaration of Independence. I make no claim to being a historian of the American Revolution, but Clinton Rossiter, another late Cornell professor who did make that claim, wrote of the revolutionary era that "it is impossible to discover an important American author who wrote in defense of 'the right of revolution.'" This should not surprise us because, according to the *Oxford English Dictionary*, the earliest use of the phrase was about 1848.

Something in the Declaration does seem to advocate a right to revolution, however, and we should not quibble about words when we are talking about profound political matters on which the safety and happiness of billions of people may depend. Let me quote the familiar passage to you, so that we all have the sound of it in our ears again, and then I will try to explain what I think its argument is:

We hold these truths to be self-evident, that all men are created equal, that they are endowed by their Creator with certain unalienable rights, that among these are life, liberty and the pursuit of happiness—That to secure these rights, governments are instituted among men, deriving their just powers from the consent of the governed, that whenever any form of government becomes destructive of these ends, it is the right of the people to alter or to abolish it, and to institute new government.

There is one more similar sentence we ought to hear again:

But when a long train of abuses and usurpations, pursuing invariably the same object, evinces a design to reduce them under absolute despotism, it is their right, it is their duty, to throw off such government, and to provide new guards for their future security.

"The right of the people to alter or abolish" "any form of government" is what Becker and others take as indicating a right of revolution. My purpose is to show that "the right of the people to alter or abolish" is fundamentally different from the right of revolution and that this right of the people, properly understood, not only does not go out of vogue after a successful revolution but has a continuing and indispensable role to play in perpetuating limited constitutional government.

To understand "the right of the people to alter or abolish," we must understand what the Declaration means by "rights," "the people," and "government." Let me start with the last.

The Absence of Government

To understand what Jefferson and other sons of Locke meant by government, we must consider men and women as they are in an ungoverned situation, living together or in contact with one another in the absence of government. Many of us resist this idea as far-fetched or even impossible, because all of us were born in political society and cannot conceive what it would be like to live without government or even that it is possible for human beings to live together without government. I understand what they have in mind when they make this objection; yet I would respond by assuring you that all of you know many very eminent people who live in an ungoverned situation with other men and women. I will also show that all of you have yourselves experienced directly the ungoverned life.

The heads of independent governments are, in relation to one another, in an ungoverned situation because, as "civilized" as many of them are, they do not have a common superior on earth with authority to judge between them in cases of disagreement. This may seem to us more evident when President John Kennedy met with Secretary Nikita Khrushchev, but that is only because there was evidence of hostility and danger when those two met. It is as true that they are in an ungoverned situation when President Gerald Ford meets with President Valéry Giscard d'Estaing or Prime Minister James Callaghan, despite the warm cordiality, because there is no superior they have consented to have authority to settle controversies that might arise between them.

The absence of government between heads of sovereign governments is one vicarious experience we all have of nongovernment, which, I remind you, is important to understand if we wish to understand what the Declaration means by government. But we not only know, distantly, others who live in an ungoverned situation, we all have direct experience of it ourselves.

All of us have had an experience like walking on a dark and deserted street, with no homes nearby or other people around and no way of calling the police in time in case we need them, when a figure suddenly approaches out of the distance. This is a no-government situation because there will be no superior with authority to act in time in case of controversy. I assume that everyone has, at some time, been in a situation like this—perhaps not with a stranger but with someone he knew or thought he knew well; perhaps not on a street but in some remote and isolated place in the country; perhaps not even in the dark but in bright and broad daylight; nevertheless, where he felt himself outside the reach of the protection of authority. If I am right that this is part of the experience of all of us, then no one is without experience of no-government; everyone knows directly what it is like to be among other persons without government.

In that ungoverned situation, we feel danger, uncertainty, insecurity, whether it is warranted or not, because without the protection of authority, force is too likely to be used by others against us without our consent, without respect for our rights. When force is used without right or authority, a kind of war is made on us, to injure or kill or at least to coerce us. The ungoverned situation need not be a coercive situation, depending on who the persons are and what the conditions of their being together are, but it is plain that an ungoverned situation becomes coercive more easily than a governed situation—or, to put it more plainly, a bully is more likely to try to coerce someone when the police are not there.

Under government the coercive activity of the Al Capone gang, for example, can and does occur, but there is at least a prospect of bringing it to an end. In an ungoverned situation such coercion is likely to end only in total surrender or death. The ungoverned situation is very unsafe, very insecure, very inconvenient, and not to be endured, even if we assume that just about everyone, but not everyone, is by nature inclined to be cooperative and peaceable.

Natural Rights

The assumption of the Declaration is that every human being is born with natural rights that are not bestowed by any human effort. The Creator, or nature's God, endows us with rights, equally. These rights are the starting point of government, but they are not political rights. The rights to life, liberty, and the pursuit of happiness are divine or natural gifts, not in the capacity of any political or governmental institution to bestow.

We start life, every one of us, according to the Declaration, with the right to life, with the liberty to protect and enhance that life, and with the right to make the best of that life. Governments are instituted by men; rights are not.

The purpose of government is to secure these rights. To do that, government must have powers to act, for example, to thwart the nonpolitical, coercive powers of criminals. Not all power is political. The powers of gangsters over victims, of parents over children, of one spouse over another, of a professor over students, of a religious leader over followers, of a boss over employees, or of a slave owner over slaves differ among themselves, and all differ from political power in many ways, although similarities make it difficult, sometimes, to distinguish them from one another.

Political powers derive from the consent of the people. In an ungoverned situation, because everyone has a right to life and the liberty to protect it, everyone has the right to resist coercion or force in the absence of authority. That means that you can fight someone who attacks you and even kill him, if you must, to save yourself from injury or death. When many persons agree to establish a common authority to secure protection for their rights, they must give up the right to take the law into their own hands and turn over that task to the authorities. This turned-over power, which was the natural right of each person in an ungoverned situation, becomes the political power of the governed. Further, by agreeing to have a common authority to judge their controversies, the many persons make themselves into one society and, instead of many individual persons,

49

become "the people." The power to punish those who attack the rights of others is turned over wholly to the people, to the society, and, through the laws they make and consent to, to the government.

Some things, however, cannot be turned over completely to the society or the government—the power of a man to judge that he personally is in danger and the right to defend himself when there is no authority to help him. This is not a matter of fiat; it is a matter of fact. If a knife is held at a man's throat, he cannot be persuaded or commanded not to feel fear; and if he feels fear, he cannot be commanded to ignore his safety and not act in whatever way seems most appropriate to protect his life. This right to act to preserve his life in extreme circumstances is not given over to the society, because it cannot be. In that sense it is inalienable. The difference between the governed and the ungoverned situation is that such dangers are more rare under a government of laws and authority; but if the rare danger does arise, the right of self-defense is inalienable, and the individual will act to save himself, naturally.

Tyranny

This leads us directly to the subject of tyranny, for the tyrant or the absolute despot, mentioned over and over again in the Declaration, is very much like the man with a knife at his victim's throat or like Al Capone's gang coercing people by force or the threat of force. The main point to understand, for an understanding of the line of argument of the Declaration, is that the power of the tyrant is not political power. Political power is made up of the powers given up by consent of the governed. The tyrant uses power that no one in his right mind would consent to give up. A tyrant uses the kind of power that Al Capone used—absolute, arbitrary power. Secret police, arrest without charge or explanation, prisoners held without trial, persons deprived of life, liberty, or property without due process of law, no choice of the persons who have power or the duration or scope of their powers—all of these are marks of powers that are not political, that are not consistent with government, because persons could not have consented to alienate such inalienable rights to anyone.

There are many examples, of course, of governments such as Hitler's Germany or present-day military dictatorships or theocratic regimes that do the things I say cannot be done by governments. But if we adhere to the Declaration's definition of governments, that they seek to secure the rights of life, liberty, and the pursuit of happiness and that their powers are derived from the consent of the governed, then those so-called governments are not governments.

To understand the possibility of governments that are not governments it is helpful to recall the story of Odysseus and the Cyclops. When asked his name, Odysseus said his name was No-Man. After the Cyclops was blinded by Odysseus and screamed for help to capture his tormentor, he was asked who had done this to him, and he replied, "No-Man"; so his would-be helpers in the chase went away.

If you think of no-form-of-government-at-all in the way you think of No-Man, that is, as something that definitely exists and acts, then you will understand that the argument of the Declaration not only acknowledges the existence, it describes in considerable detail the power exercised by no-form-of-government-at-all parading as government.

Perhaps Thomas Jefferson would allow, for the purpose of showing more clearly what the Declaration really means, the impiety of adding some words to it. After the sentence saying that governments are instituted to secure our rights, it would be clearer if it went on as follows:

> That whenever any form of government becomes destructive of these ends, *it ceases to be government and becomes no-form-of-government-at-all, and* it is the right of the people to alter or to abolish it, and to institute new government.

The later sentence should also read as follows:

> But when a long train of abuses . . . evinces a design to reduce them under absolute despotism, it is their right, it is their duty, to throw off such *non-government parading as* government, and to provide new guards for their future security.

The authors of the Declaration would not deny that some people live under tyranny; they would deny that that is government. Those people are under some kind of power, but it is not political power. Locke has a brief and blunt way of expressing this point. When a king becomes a tyrant and uses force without right against the people, for his benefit instead of theirs, Locke says, "The king has dethroned himself." The king is no king.

The people who come under the power of a tyrant do not have government. The tyrant is subject to no law; since he and his subjects do not have a common superior on earth to judge between them, he and they are in an ungoverned situation in relation to each other. This is worse than the dark street, because at least there one has some fighting chance in a one-against-one confrontation if it comes to that; besides, one has some chance by running. But the odds against us are

51

overwhelming when we are faced by a tyrant; so we are worse off under no-government tyranny than in an ungoverned situation.

The argument of the Declaration, then, is not revolutionary in the sense that it speaks of a right to overthrow governments. Rather it is a strongly progovernment argument that urges the right to have government no matter what the odds and obstacles. It addresses itself to the greatest obstacle, the existence of tyranny, the existence of a sham government that is powerful and destructive of the chief purposes of true government. It argues that in the face of no-form-of-government-at-all—this most powerful imaginable antigovernment force, not only overbearing but deceitfully disguised as government itself—the people have a right, the people have a duty, to get rid of it so that they can have government.

If we turn again to the Declaration, we see that the part usually called the "bill of particulars" follows the argument I have just outlined. The object of the king of Great Britain is "establishment of an absolute tyranny over these States." He has obstructed legislation, he has denied representation, he has dissolved legislatures, and so on, concluding with the words, "He has abdicated government here, by declaring us out of his protection and waging war against us. . . . A Prince, whose character is thus marked by every act which may define a tyrant, is unfit to be the ruler of a free people." In short, the king is no king, certainly no king of ours.

The right to alter or abolish a nongovernment that becomes destructive of the ends of government is different from the other rights spoken of in the Declaration. Life, liberty, and the pursuit of happiness are rights of every person. The right to alter or abolish is the right of "the people," not of individuals. How do the people judge that the king has unkinged himself, that the government is no-government-at-all and therefore needs to be altered or abolished and a new government instituted? There is no procedure and can be none within the laws, because this right of the people is effective only when the law or the constitution itself is perverted and becomes the enemy of the rights of the individual citizens. This may be a difficult determination for lawyers and political scientists to make, but they are not the judges: the people shall be judge whether the government has become tyrannical and ceased to be the government whose authority they consented to. The people can be trusted, the Declaration assures us, not to make the judgment hastily or rashly: "all experience hath shewn, that mankind are more disposed to suffer, while evils are sufferable, than to right themselves by abolishing the forms to which they are accustomed."

I think we can say, with Jefferson, 200 years later, that the experience of mankind is still the same, that people in too many lands put up with vicious government that we, and other free peoples, would find intolerable and would not stand for. I mean things like a press owned and controlled by the government, sham elections, political arrest and detention, secret trials, denial of the freedom to emigrate, interrogation by torture, and so on in a long and horrendous list that would include before we finished the official murder of millions of their own people.

Conclusion

The people in some nations put up with violations of their rights that the people of other nations would not tolerate. That is a greater danger to the safety and well-being of mankind than the opposite danger that the people will rise up frivolously with the cry of tyranny on their lips "for light and transient reasons." That brings me to the concluding thought of this analysis, the importance to the nation and to the world of understanding the true meaning and continuing significance of the Declaration of Independence, especially the contribution to stable good government that results from grasping the meaning of "the right of the people to alter or abolish."

The people of a nation that has the lesson of the Declaration in its bones, as the people of the United States have, will always be on the alert for dangers to their rights. They will be unusually alert because they will have many fences built around their rights, fences that both defend and warn. At the center is life itself. Around it is liberty, liberty of action to defend life. Around the liberty of each person is property, not only material goods but the freedom to acquire them. Around those is the pursuit of happiness, which requires a freedom of action in many activities other than earning a living. The rings of fences protecting our rights reach out rather far, so that a patriotic American bred on the doctrine of the Declaration feels the danger when he hears that there is a tax imposed by a legislature in which he was not represented, as if it were a threat to his life. His system of warning fences conveys the message that if they can do that, what can they not do?

Other people in other lands, less well trained in the lessons of the Declaration, are amazed that so much can be made of such a minor matter as a tax on tea. But the Americans know that a tax without representation threatens their property, because taxes thus levied can be confiscatory; and that property gives independence of action and is thus a fence around liberty; and that liberty of action is essential for self-preservation. So, in a flash, just as long as it takes for an impulse to travel the nervous system from the toe that has been stepped on to the brain that feels the pain and the vocal cords that emit the cry, the American knows that that tax on tea endangers his life and that he ought to protest.

"Prudence, indeed, will dictate that government long established should not be changed for light and transient reasons," and that has been the American experience since 1789. But what has helped make this the world's oldest fundamentally unchanged form of government is the alertness of the citizenry to violations of their rights and the corresponding alertness of government officials to the right the people have to act if they feel their rights are seriously violated. Tyranny will begin to retreat in the world only as this lesson, clearly and prudently set forth, is spread throughout the world.

It would be a blessing if somehow the mistaken teachings about the Declaration disseminated in Becker's book could be dispelled and replaced by an appreciation of the difference between a right of revolution and the right to resist tyranny. It would make a very great difference if it were widely understood that the right to resist tyranny was, and is, the founding principle of our constitutional government, so stable that it has persisted long enough to celebrate its 200th anniversary.

PART TWO
Rights—Brief, Negative, and Duty Free

7

Rights versus Duties

The question is asked why more cannot be done, why more is not done, to encourage a sense of citizen obligation in the United States, to accompany and balance the strong urge evidenced by all elements of the population to demand their rights. Why cannot we Americans be more considerate of the rights of others and more willing to sacrifice for the good of the country, instead of concentrating, as we do, on the self-interested pursuit of personal and group advantage?

Rights and Duties in Everyday Life

In our everyday lives rights and duties are clearly linked. That every right has a reciprocal duty is the sort of thing "everybody knows." In family life, for example, the connection between rights and duties is so obvious that adults expect very young children to understand it. This has been true in all societies and at all times down through history, as far as one can judge from plays, stories, accounts of travelers, folk tales, and even historical, sociological, and anthropological studies.

In any society, including ours, where there is private family life, it is commonly understood that what might be called the right of a child to be fed a cooked meal by the mother entails some kind of corresponding duty—to help set the table or clear it, wash the dishes or put them away, or some other related task. If it is a rural family, then the chores that go with picking vegetables or collecting eggs or chopping wood are the commonly understood duties. (That a guest in one's home has no such obligation to help, although help may be volunteered, is a sign of special exemption, distinguishing the unobliged guest from the obliged family members. The outsider, after all, has no right to be at the table, in the way that a son or daughter has, but only an invitation.)

A child may resist doing his duty; he may disobey; the parent may not require fulfillment of the child's duty. Yet the connection between the right and the duty is so obvious that all adults expect any child to be able to understand, with little or no explanation, that the benefit has a price, that the privilege is but half of a balanced relationship essential to a decent and viable familial society, that rights and duties are inextricable.

The same is true in relationships among friends, neighbors, associates, colleagues, and even strangers who must deal with each other. It is true that many people have the habit of taking advantage of others, of acting on the maxim that "what is yours is mine and what is mine is mine," but that is considered a bad habit, and people who develop it are criticized, complained about, and scorned for it. Whatever we may do when we are looking out for ourselves at the expense of others (and probably all of us do so at one time or another), almost none of us disputes that the general rule is and ought to be that one is obliged to reciprocate and that duties and rights, privileges and obligations extend equally.

One may claim rights without acknowledging duties, just as one may take goods from a store without paying, by stealth or fraud or force, but there is no great difficulty, in common sense and in moral theory, in recognizing the wrongness of doing it and the evil of trying to justify it. Theft is theft, whether of goods or of rights. There is honor among thieves, as the saying goes; even they know that taking without reciprocal giving cannot be the basis of amicable human association.

I have used these simple arguments and homely examples because at the level of personal and family relationships the issues are truly simple—which is usually not the same as saying they are easy to grasp. (Elements are harder to detect and fathom than combinations of them. Scholars and others who are at their best in studying complexities often make their most profound errors at the elementary level.) But if I am right in saying that rights and obligations have an obvious and universal and, one might say, natural connection, what, then, is the problem? Why should anyone raise a question about the connection between political rights and the obligations of citizens?

My answer is that political rights are different from the rights I have been speaking of. The political situation is very different from the familial and social ones. With regard to rights and duties in the political context, all is not as it seems, not as one would expect, not as any child can understand. My argument is that in political society it is essential to liberty that rights and duties *not* be directly linked in the law.

In the rest of this essay, I will try to explain the hidden trap in the question about the connection between rights and duties of citizens. My advice to anyone who cares seriously about protecting the rights of the people, when asked what duties are owed to society in exchange for the rights enjoyed, is a clear imperative: "Don't answer that question!" Exercise your right to remain silent until the question is reformulated. There is a good answer, as I will try to show, but not to that question.

Rights and Duties in Political Societies

It may be too much to ask of citizens that their political credo be "one for all and all for one," but surely the *esprit* of any political society that hopes to persist must be somewhat closer to that than to "every man for himself." A society of any kind—from the Three Musketeers to a mass of hundreds of millions—can achieve the cohesion that makes individuals into a society only if there is a widely shared concern regarding what is good or harmful for the group or community as a whole. And since any human society is made up of individuals who can think for themselves—as distinguished from, say, social insects such as ants, bees, or termites—there is a fundamental problem.

Individuals who have the ability and inclination to calculate what is good for themselves as individuals or for themselves as part of a smaller group (family, religious sect, ethnic group, special trade or business) within the larger community (neighborhood, city, nation, international alliance) unavoidably generate a tension between the personal or partial or partisan interest and the interest of the society as a whole.

The conflict between private interests and the public interest is inevitable in any political society, no matter what its character or form of government; societies differ, however, sometimes strikingly, in the methods they use to cope with or forestall or eliminate this conflict.

Many political societies have tried to prevent or minimize the conflict of private interests and the public good by education or indoctrination. Some have used myths, such as that the original founders of the community all sprang from the native soil and therefore all its citizens have an indissoluble bond of responsibility to one another as brothers and sisters, or that the ruler presides by some ancient act of divine designation and right and that obedience is therefore owed, as to the gods. Others use a combination of force and organization along military lines to turn the whole society into a disciplined group resembling an army, so that the safety of each seems linked to the strength of the whole. Ancient Sparta, we learn from Plutarch, was made into such a society by a sudden and drastic land reform that eliminated inequalities of wealth; a currency reform, making lead the only legal tender, that made commerce and foreign trade impossible; and a decree that everyone had to eat in military-style dining clubs, which ended the softening influences of mother, family, home, and kitchen. On this constitutional foundation, it was possible to make all Spartans think of themselves as soldiers who put the good of the city ahead of personal concerns. That Spartan regime overcame many enemies and lasted for more than 600 years.

Other societies have attempted to achieve a sense of public duty through indoctrination, patriotism, inculcating love of the fatherland through a teaching of the national or racial or religious superiority of the tribe or sect or city or nation. We are all familiar with the practice in our personal experience, both the advantages and the dangers, through related phenomena known as school spirit or team spirit or, in military units, *esprit de corps*. It almost invariably has two aspects: (1) a cohesion developed by a sense of common aspiration or a common danger or shared superiority or *something* to set this group off from all others as distinctive and exclusive; and (2) strong disapproval of concern for individual benefit at the expense of others in the group and strong approval of group loyalty and personal sacrifice for the sake of the group.

Of course there are numerous examples of force and terror to bring about behavior that serves the group at the expense of personal comfort and safety, although, even in the most horrifying cases, force is usually combined with other efforts. In Nazi Germany, for example, assertion of personal rights at the expense of the national purpose was physically dangerous if not suicidal; but terror and force were not relied on alone. Relentless propaganda and indoctrination were frighteningly successful. Allegiance to the Nazi cause and to Hitler's leadership was not only strong but fanatically so. The standard of citizen obligation was extraordinarily high, despicable though it was.

In a very different regime with different principles and aims, we have seen on television disciplined troupes of Iranian men flagellating themselves with heavy chains to display their devotion on a special holy day to a leader and to a cause above self. In watching them and appraising the sight, one must keep in mind that to do what these groups were doing in such precise rhythmic unison surely took months of repetitive rehearsal, as is common in our military drill teams and high school cheerleading squads. In short, they must devote a significant part of their lives training to beat themselves with chains, not just one day a year. Such denial of self for a common cause is as impressive as it is frightening.

A willingness to subordinate private to public ends must be inculcated, one way or another, in any society. The results are often amazing. The self-denial of some peoples, their self-discipline or disciplined obedience to others, their selflessness, their devotion to a cause, their readiness to sacrifice their means and even their lives impress us and often win our admiration. And yet, keeping the preceding examples in mind, we must have doubts about the methods used and the purposes served. Those examples remind us that regimes frequently use abhorrent methods to overcome the disruptive force of selfish assertion of rights. We also see that regimes seek to form the character of their citizens to suit the way they want the society to be constituted and that not all the regimes are admirable or consistent with political freedom, to say the least.

Every society seeks to make good citizens. Good citizens are attentive to the good of the society as a whole; that is, they do their public duty. But as Aristotle pointed out long ago, good citizens are not necessarily good men. A good man will not be a good citizen in an evil regime. The most admirable human beings in Hitler's Germany and Brezhnev's Soviet Union were recognized as bad citizens and treated accordingly by imprisonment, exile, or execution. Solzhenitsyn loved his homeland, but he was not a good Soviet citizen.

A good man has less trouble being a good citizen in a good regime; but as even the best of actual political societies will have flaws and make demands that require conformity and will often be foolish and sometimes wicked, the better the man, the more reluctant and qualified his devotion must be to some of the demands of citizenship. That observation brings us to the special difficulty that a *free* society has in dealing with the conflict of private rights and public duty. It seems easier for a military regime to deal with this conflict, or a fascist dictatorship or a dictatorship of the proletariat or a theocracy or a monarchy based on divine right. Each in its own way compels a certain behavior. But how can a free society proceed, especially one that is based on the *primacy* of the rights of the individual? Selfishness must be restrained or overcome in one way or another. Because the tendency to serve self-interest is strong, all regimes must find a way to cope with it; but other regimes do not have the problem faced by a liberal democracy because only the latter elevates the right to pursue self-interest to a fundamental principle of government.

Not all regimes go to the lengths of Mao's China or Khomeini's Iran in discouraging the pursuit of self-interest, but few also go out of their way to encourage that pursuit. Where the personal rights of life, liberty, property, and the pursuit of happiness are the starting point for all political thought and action, there is obviously a special problem of reconciling private rights and public duty.

61

Self-Preservation, the Foundation of Rights

What are natural rights, and how do we know we have them? The doctrine of natural rights is based on a view of human nature and a theory of the origin of political society, and as political theories go it is a quite modern teaching. Ancient writers such as Plato and Aristotle did not speak about rights, although they thought and wrote about political matters in an extraordinarily comprehensive way. To the best of my knowledge the Bible does not speak of rights; as we would expect, biblical teachings, old and new, are concerned with our duties to God, not rights that we might claim.

The natural rights teachings of authors like Thomas Hobbes, John Locke, and Jean-Jacques Rousseau start with a description of men as being naturally free, independent of one another, equal, and without government. In their book, man is not a citizen by nature, not a part of a *polis* or any political community by nature. Instead, the natural state of man is to be without government. Aristotle had said that it is not possible to be human outside a *polis;* one would be a brute or a god, but not a man. That is the meaning of his assertion that man is a political animal. Political community, in that view, is a necessary condition for the full development of human qualities; without political community we are unfinished, less than human, unnaturally stunted, short of the natural human completion.

Hobbes, Locke, and Rousseau took man as being in his natural state outside civil society. Locke, for example, considering what the human condition would be in that state of nature, argued that men have certain natural rights that are theirs and cannot be taken away: life, principally; the liberty necessary to defend that life; and the property or means to sustain it. Life, liberty, and property are the basic natural rights. (It was Jefferson's innovation to substitute "the pursuit of happiness," although that phrase, too, was Locke's.) What makes these rights basic is that they all stem from the desire for self-preservation.

The desire for self-preservation is the most powerful human desire, according to Locke. You cannot be persuaded that you are doing wrong, no matter how far you go, if you are protecting yourself against unprovoked, violent, deadly attack. And if it is impossible to persuade you that it is wrong, you know you are right, you know you have the right to defend yourself even if you must kill an aggressor. The desire for self-preservation, private and basic, is the not-very-lofty source of human rights.

The consequences of this teaching, basic to the American Constitution and to our advocacy of human rights, are manifold. The individual human being is naturally free and independent and only artificially a citizen. The natural state of man is to be free of any control to which he has not freely given his consent. All men are equal in their rights (because they are all equally desirous of self-preservation). Political society and government are legitimate only if the governed have consented to the limits imposed on individual freedom by law. Finally, the powers of government are limited to those necessary to protect life, liberty, property, and the pursuit of happiness—and that means that there are many powers that are not truly *political* powers, that cannot legitimately be exercised unless it can be shown that doing so serves to secure the rights of the people.

These are the grounds for talking about natural rights, or human rights, or inalienable rights, or rights of any name. Societies based on notions of man as a citizen by nature (that is, the *polis* as the natural state of man) or by divine decree (that is, a theocracy that makes duty to God the principal source of law and society's institutions) may be superior to ours. They may nurture finer human qualities and more dutiful and more virtuous citizens, but in such societies it makes no sense to speak of the natural rights of the people. In such societies a citizen is granted permission to act as necessary to perform his duties to state or church. What would be in a free society the right to read anything becomes in a *polis* or a theocracy a duty to read everything necessary to fulfill one's obligations to society and to read nothing that would interfere with those obligations.

A government or church that controls the reading material of citizens or church members of every rank may forbid most to read the very writings they require a few others to study with great care, so that all can think and do what is best for the well-being of the society as a whole, whether it be prosperity on earth or the salvation of eternal souls. The presumption against censorship does not exist in all societies, but only in those whose principle is the primacy of the individual and his basic rights. It may not be the loftiest platform for asserting the right of free speech, but it is a solid one, to argue that a man can rightly assume that rulers who want to silence him may be doing so because they have in mind to deprive him of his liberty and perhaps even of his life. The right to speak about issues that affect one's life, liberty, property, or happiness can also be traced back to the strongest desire—that of self-preservation.

Pitting Rights against Rights

The United States was the first nation explicitly founded on the principle of the primacy and equality of natural human rights, and the founders were aware that such a nation has a special problem in promoting the kind of dutiful citizenship necessary for justice, good order, and prosperity. The method they devised, through the Constitution, to encourage good citizenship was an innovation, a practical if not a theoretical one.

The theoretical problem is difficult in itself and intimidating. Simply stated, it comes down to this: if the rights of citizens are derived from the single most powerful human desire, then rights are natural and powerful. No one needs to be exhorted to exercise these basic natural rights. But looking at the other side of it, if political society is artificial, a man-made entity, and man is not a citizen by nature, then our sense of duty to that society is not natural and will not be powerful enough to stand in opposition to natural rights. When it comes to pitting private rights *against* public obligations, the outcome must inevitably be no contest in a society whose citizens are educated in the doctrines of natural rights and whose institutions reinforce these doctrines.

How can the undue exercise of private rights be restrained in a society based on the primacy of private rights? The "new science of politics," proclaimed by the authors of the Constitution in *The Federalist*, is forthright and direct: pit private rights against private rights, let "ambition counteract ambition." Only the desire to exercise one's rights is strong enough, in the free society they envisaged, to oppose and restrain the free—but socially dangerous—exercise of the rights of others. It is in this way, they said, that "the private interest of every individual may be a sentinel over the public rights."[1]

The American solution to the age-old conflict of private rights and public duties was not to speak of obligations but to develop a certain character and behavior of citizens by designing a regime with institutions that encourage the pursuit of private advantage through public activity. The founders had in mind town councils, state legislatures, jury duty, voting for local, state, and federal officials, lobbying, organizing interest groups—all those activities that often make private-sector and public-sector activities almost indistinguishable and certainly inseparable. Experience in the exercise of political rights would habituate the self-seeking individual in behavior that was moderate, considerate of others, conciliatory, civil, and compromising, very much like that of a truly public-spirited citizen. A man who firmly believes that "honesty is the best policy" and is honest in his dealings for the sake of policy rather than for the sake of honesty will be, in his visible actions and habits, indistinguishable from the man who is honest for the sake of honesty.

The American constitutional scheme, as described by Madison and others, does not seek to balance rights and duties, nor does it encourage talk about rights versus duties. Rights are too likely to win out in every such contest. Only rights have a sufficient natural power to counter rights successfully. The discourse of the founders is full of talk about the rights and interests of the people and of the community as a whole but nearly silent about duties, although most of them, admirably and honorably, some even gloriously, devoted themselves to public service at very considerable personal sacrifice and risk of time, money, health, and life itself. They made clear what they were risking when they pledged to each other, at the end of the Declaration of Independence, "our lives, our fortunes, and our sacred honor."

How Are Rights Secured in America?

If my argument is correct, the protection of rights has a double importance in this country and in any other similarly constituted: the exercise of our rights is essential not only to personal liberty but also to the common good. The power of individuals and groups to act freely in their own interest is a safeguard, perhaps ultimately the chief safeguard, of the public interest.

How are rights best protected? The answer an American is most likely to give is, "by the Bill of Rights," or for many other countries, "by the power of world public opinion." I will examine both these answers, but first it is important to observe that the question, What truly serves to protect our rights? is rarely asked today. For some reason it is not considered to require serious thought. In contrast, it was considered a question of paramount importance by Madison, and some of his best writing was devoted to it. Much of the superficiality of human rights doctrine today and much of the futility of human rights activism are related, I think, to the failure to ask and to ponder seriously this question.

The *Federalist* papers were written in 1787–1788 as part of the effort to ensure ratification of the new Constitution in the state of New York. They are a detailed commentary on the Constitution with one persistent theme: that the chief purpose of the government to be established under the Constitution is to secure the rights of the people. But we must remind ourselves that at the time these papers were being written the Constitution did not contain the Bill of Rights; it was added, as everyone knows, in 1791, as the first ten amendments to the Constitution. Madison, therefore, in writing on this subject in *Federalist* No. 51 could not have given the answer we would now tend to give—that the Bill of Rights is what secures the rights of the people. How was the argument made that the Constitution without the Bill of Rights secures the rights of the people?

In fact, in the body of the Constitution the word "right" occurs only once, in the provision known as the copyright and patent clause, and there it is clear that "the exclusive right" of authors and inventors to benefit from "their writings and discoveries" is not a natural right. In other words, the document that Madison claimed was designed to protect the rights of the citizens did not even mention such rights, let alone guarantee their free exercise.

Madison's answer to the question—What truly protects rights?— follows from the principles of a free society: that rights are primary, that only rights are strong enough to restrain and control rights, and that the public good is best served by the habits developed by citizens exercising their rights in opposition to other citizens doing the same. "In a free government," Madison says,

> the security for civil rights must be the same as that for religious rights. It consists in the one case in the multiplicity of interests, and in the other in the multiplicity of sects. The degree of security in both cases will depend on the number of interests and sects.[2]

Madison later became the chief author of the First Amendment and would now no doubt agree that it is a powerful force in protecting our civil and religious rights; yet I doubt that he would modify his argument that the more interest groups we have and the more religious sects we have, the more security there is for civil and religious liberty. He might contend that the First Amendment continues to be effective in protecting rights (though similar provisions are ineffective in other countries) in large part because of the multiplicity of American interest groups and religious sects. He might even argue that one of the most important consequences of the First Amendment has been the encouragement it affords to the increase in the number of interest groups and religious sects. And he might add that even with the First Amendment religious freedom would be in great jeopardy in this country, as in many others, if at some time *any* religious sect became dominant.

Much of the design of the institutions established under the Constitution has as its aim multiplying the interests and allowing them to assert themselves. The scheme of representation, for example, gives voice to a tremendous diversity of interests, giving them every chance to compete and yet making it difficult, if not impossible, for one to dominate as a persisting majority.

66

There is little that is morally satisfying in this formulation. Madison had no illusions, for instance, about disinterested congressmen with nothing in their minds but the common interest. We all know that it is wrong for any man to judge in his own cause; but, Madison asked, "What are the different classes of legislators but advocates and parties to the causes which they determine?"[3] There may be forces of moral excellence or religious restraint seeking to protect our rights, but we cannot rely on them. There is, in fact, the opposite assumption: that Americans are human beings and not angels, and when given the chance they are very likely to take advantage of others and violate their rights.

Even with our doctrine of the primacy of rights, the Constitution, the Bill of Rights, the separation of powers and federalism, and the multiplicity of interests and sects, the whole history of American legislation and litigation—federal, state, and local—is nevertheless one long procession of groups and individuals struggling to deprive other groups and individuals of their rights. The best we can say for ourselves—and it is indeed a lot to say—is that our principles, laws, and institutions are almost all arrayed on the side of securing rights and against the efforts to violate them. In that struggle what we have been habituated to rely on is not a disinterested self-restraint but the energetic pursuit of self-interest by others, if they are equally free, and the clash of interests and ambitions where there are enough competitors and none with an overwhelming and persisting concentration of power.

The expectation is that the clash of interests and ambitions will be guided, constrained, and ultimately transformed by the regular procedural channels that have been established by the Constitution for passing, executing, and interpreting the laws of the land. Those procedural pathways force some sort of mutual accommodation among the crudest forms of interest and ambition, and over time such accommodation, compromise, and mutual consideration become habitual. The result is behavior perhaps distinguishable from but yet very similar to that of restrained, considerate, public-spirited citizens.

The adequacy of such a citizenry to meet every test is doubtful. Patriotism, obviously, can be relied on only when the public danger is great enough to affect all or most private concerns, as when the nation is attacked by powerful enemies. But the response to a peacetime draft will be doubtful, that is, to demands for personal sacrifice when the national danger is neither clear nor present. And in matters less immediate than military danger, such as an energy shortage, it seems clear that for Americans there is no moral equivalent of war; energy conservation can be achieved by a price increase, but not by moral exhortation.

No lover of liberty should be willing to repeal the First Amendment, but we should be clear that by itself it cannot protect our rights of religion, speech, press, assembly, and petition. The Soviet Constitution, to give only one example of scores of constitutions that could be cited, has a list of rights that includes all those in the Bill of Rights and many, many more, and in addition *guarantees* those rights in a way that our Constitution does not attempt; yet we know that the exercise of the rights of religion, speech, press, petition, and assembly in the Soviet Union is very insecure.

Words on paper cannot secure rights unless they are buttressed by a certain ordering of the institutions, the society, and the economy of the nation. The written Constitution must correspond to the way the nation is truly constituted. If it does not, its protections of rights are a mere "parchment barrier," easily shredded by malevolent (or even by benevolent) forces. In any nation where there is a tremendous concentration of economic and political power and no diversity of interests and religious sects, the most that can be hoped for in human rights is a few minor concessions in individual cases when, for one reason or another of policy, it suits the advantage of those in power to make those concessions. But there can be no internal basis for security of rights—and exhortation or moral fervor will be ineffective. Madison put the point this way: "We well know that neither moral nor religious motives can be relied on as an adequate control."[4] He urged instead the "policy of supplying by opposite and rival interests, the defect of better motives."[5]

The Danger of Linking Rights and Duties

A free political society based on the primacy of rights cannot be fully satisfying to those whose hopes are for a nation founded on the loftiest principles and devoted to the development of the finest qualities of human nature. But even those who feel these lacks most keenly have no choice but to reconcile themselves to the sad fact that it is not just the United States, not just the Western liberal democracies, but modernity in its full flowering, with its roots in the Renaissance, that puts us in the position I have described.

We do not have a choice between our natural rights doctrine and some other kinds of government based on ancient teachings of virtue, justice, and nobility characteristic of political philosophy before Machiavelli. The choice is limited either to what we and other liberal democracies have—a great degree of political liberty for most citizens, along with material prosperity (despite ups and downs) unprecedented in the history of the world—or to the alternatives that we see about us in a hostile and hateful world: Marxist dictatorships, military dictatorships, racist regimes, underdeveloped economies suffering in unspeakable ignorance and penury, theocratic tyrannies, and so on in a long catalog of political, economic, and social horrors.

At some point in the course of our long list of complaints about the undoubted defects of our political, economic, social, and moral institutions and principles we must eventually face up to the vulgar but sobering question, Compared to what? On the very question of this essay—the linking of citizen duties to private rights as a means of restraining and civilizing the ceaseless clashing, struggling, striving to outdo each other, the din, clamor, and turmoil—could we not try *something* to strengthen our sense of duty, of obligation to our fellow citizens and to society as a whole? Why can't we at least try to imagine a constitution that would do that?

To return to the homely example I began with, is it really out of the question that in our Constitution, or somewhere, we could say that it is the policy of this people that "children are obliged to show concern for their parents and to help them"? And to deal with the suffering of people who cannot find a place to live, guarantee them the right to housing, and at the same time to deal with one of the abuses that is so evident in all of our cities, provide that "citizens must take good care of the housing allocated to them"? And since there are, similarly, two major problems having to do with employment, on the one hand many who cannot find a job and on the other hand many who do not conscientiously look for a job, why not proclaim that "citizens have the right to labor—that is, to receive guaranteed work and remuneration" and tie it to the duty of working in "socially useful activity"?

To ensure basic freedoms and at the same time to try to restrain irresponsible excesses of the mass media, we could consider, although it might be going too far, linking "guaranteed freedom of speech, of the press, of assembly" to the duty of using those rights only "in accordance with the people's interests and for the purpose of strengthening and developing" the system of government. But in stead, perhaps we could devise a briefer and more comprehensive provision and not go into so many details—something like, "The exercise of rights and liberties is inseparable from the performance by citizens of their duties."

If those are all things we believe in, why not put them down in law and see if that does not have the same constructive and formative effect in making the citizenry duties-conscious that our centuries-long emphasis on rights has so obviously had in making us rights-conscious?

At this point I urge the attentive reader to recall the advice given in the beginning of this essay that questions about linking rights and duties should not be answered, certainly not hastily. All the suggested provisions for an "imagined" constitution explicitly linking duties and rights are quoted directly from the Soviet Constitution of 1977.[6] For several reasons it would be unreasonable to reject them simply because they come from an unsavory source. Many good ideas and principles are incorporated in bad contexts and do not change their nature when removed from those contexts, but their virtues become more visible. A diamond lying in a heap of dung is not garbage even while it lies in the village dump; but it is more likely to be seen to be just what it is, a precious gem, when it is removed.

The Constitution of the United States enumerates very few rights, and they are in the amendments. The Soviet Constitution enumerates all the most familiar rights—of press, speech, assembly, religion—and many more: the rights to labor, rest, health care, material security in old age, housing, education, the use of cultural achievements, participation in public affairs, and to criticize state agencies. Not only are these rights enumerated, they are guaranteed. For example:

> USSR citizens have the right to labor—that is, to receive guaranteed work and remuneration for labor in accordance with its quantity and quality and not below the minimum amount established by the state. . . . This right is ensured by the socialist economic system, [and] the steady growth of productive forces.[7]

Implicit in a guarantee of a job to every citizen, if it is at all meaningful, is the necessity for the state to control the labor market, both the supply of jobs and the supply of workers for every kind of job. No president of the United States can honestly guarantee a job to every citizen (although such wording is increasingly found in our legislation and regulations), because he does not have enough control over the economy and the labor force and hiring and firing by millions of employers. Behind the guarantee of a job to every citizen in the Soviet Union is the fact that there is really only one employer and that is the state. In the United States and in other similar nations there is a multiplicity of interests, industries, and employers all making independent decisions about hiring and firing on the basis of self-interest—that is, trying to earn a return on investment rather than on the basis of a government's judgment of what constitutes "socially useful activity."

This is a very great difference. When Alger Hiss was released from prison, he was not a popular figure with the government or with the general public, but he found a job as an executive in a small company producing women's hair ornaments. Of the more than 15 million independent enterprises in the United States, there is likely to be at least one with whom even a convicted perjurer can find employment. But in the Soviet Union, where there is only one employer, if a citizen has a falling out with that boss his plight is hopeless.

But let us keep our logic straight: the fact that there is but one employer in the Soviet Union is not the result of a guarantee of a job in the Soviet Constitution. It is the other way around: the fact that there is only one employer, the state, makes it honest and possible to guarantee a job to every citizen. Add to this that there is only one schoolmaster (guaranteed education for every citizen), only one landlord (guaranteed housing for every citizen), only one owner of travel agencies, resorts, and sports facilities (guaranteed rest and recreation for every citizen), and one begins to sense the sinister implications of a long list of constitutionally guaranteed rights of citizens. If a citizen somehow offends the only boss, the only landlord, the only schoolmaster, where will he work, where will he live, where will he be able to study?

If the list is long enough and the guarantees strong enough, the result is a tremendous accretion of power in the hands of the state, the source of these guaranteed rights. We in the United States are in the habit of speaking of the First Amendment as guaranteeing our rights of religion, speech, press, and so on, but as a matter of fact that is inaccurate, and dangerously so. The wording is strikingly different from a guarantee of rights: "Congress shall make no law . . . prohibiting the free exercise" of religion or "abridging the freedom of speech." The negative formulation is a careful denial of powers to the Congress, not a grant of powers. Furthermore, the list of rights that Congress cannot prohibit, abridge, or infringe is very short, and all are basic. The concern was, obviously, just as Madison argued in *The Federalist*:

> In framing a government which is to be administered by men over men, the great difficulty lies in this: you must first enable the government to control the governed; and in the next place oblige it to control itself.[8]

If great concentrations of power are placed in the hands of the government, enough effectively to guarantee every citizen housing, a job, education of every sort, and many other guarantees as well, nothing will be powerful enough to "oblige" the government "to control it-self"—and *that* is the obligation about which we should be most concerned if we care about liberty. Our framers had a firm grasp on a simple, ironic truth: rights are best protected by a list that is short, negative, not guaranteed, and not connected to duties.

Linking duties to rights by law goes along well with long lists of rights and guarantees of them. The rights enumerated in the Soviet Constitution are clearly seen as gifts bestowed on the citizens by the state. The Soviet Constitution is generous in giving rights to the citizens, and so it seems appropriate that there be a just price to pay for each beneficence. For the guaranteed right to a job, the duty to do useful work; for the guaranteed right to "well-appointed housing" and "low apartment rents," the duty to take good care of the housing; for the guaranteed right to freedoms of speech and press, the duty to use them "in accordance with the people's interests and for the purpose of strengthening and developing the socialist system."

But rights as we Americans understand them, natural rights, are not given to us by the state. We have them, as we have life, indepen-dent of any gift from the state. We consent to be governed on the understanding that we have entrusted no power to the state to abridge those rights. We owe nothing to the state for those rights because we did not get them from the state. The gratitude and sense of duty we may feel to the society as a whole is not so much related to our rights as to all the other sources of patriotic sentiments, which are many and powerful. But to the extent that they are related to rights, it is not for giving us the rights, but instead for helping to protect them.

The connecting of duties to rights has the following implications: that rights are bestowed by the state, which is wrong; that enjoyment of rights can be made conditional on the performance of duties and still be rights (mine *by right*, not by someone's concession), which is wrong; and that if duties are not performed, the rights can be with-drawn and still be spoken of as rights, which is wrong.

Connecting duties to rights under law is charging a price for something the state never owned, a form of selling stolen goods. As citizens we have many duties—to obey the laws, to pay our taxes, to defend the country—but however we regard these duties and how-ever we encourage their performance, it is a grave mistake to link them to the enjoyment of our rights. When duties are linked to rights by law, the rights are not just weakened, they cease to be rights as our constitutional system understands them and as we have always advo-cated them.

Conclusion

We Americans are concerned, and rightly so, about the growth of the seemingly endless and insatiable claims of rights that all parts of the citizenry want to have satisfied. At the same time, a sense of service, of duty, of concern for the rights of others, of willingness to make even small sacrifices now for the sake of the general good later—all these seem to be weak and atrophying. But in our longing for a better balance, for an improvement in *esprit* and devotion to the American cause, we must be wary of false remedies that will only make the malady, such as it is, worse.

The American scheme that has served us well, when we have understood and used it well, is fundamentally moderate and anti-utopian. We are not angels and we do not live in heaven. It is a special kind of present-day heresy to act as if our proper goal and expectation is to make a heaven on earth. Those who think so, consciously or not, run terrible risks—no less terrible for being unaware—of committing foul crimes against mankind at the worst, and of losing our liberties for us at the least.

We have the liberties we now enjoy and have enjoyed for 200 years because the founders knew the dangers of seeking guarantees for things—beautiful, highly desirable things—that cannot be guaranteed by "a government administered by men over men," that is, not angels over angels. The effort to guarantee the full, total, complete, unblemished fulfillment of freedom, prosperity, and dutifulness will lead not to the success but to the great concentrations of power in the hands of tyrants that *we see* in every country where the effort has been made.

The vice of greed is not limited to material things. There is also what might be called "moral greed," and its effects can be deadly, fatal to liberty, decency, restraint, and moderation.[9] The alternative to the greedy pursuit of an unearthly perfection of protection of every right for every person, and assurance of a strong sense of dutifulness in all of us, is a willingness to accept imperfection—because this earth is imperfect, and we human beings are imperfect, and imperfection and incompleteness and partial success/partial failure are our proper lot until we shuffle off.

Moral greed is one vice our founders did not suffer from, or suffer in others. Their whole founding effort was a rejection of that vice and a search, instead, for principles and institutions that would benefit, as much as possible, from human frailties that they did not much admire, but that they thought were so prevalent that one might better try to turn them to the benefit of mankind than try to eradicate them. For they knew from careful study and reflection on the political history of mankind up to their own time that human vice, weakness, and ugliness can be totally eradicated only by eradicating great masses of unoffending people.

Instead of seeking to establish a heaven on earth, they sought to make life freer, more decent, more comfortable, safer, and, for most people, happier. We trifle with those goals only at incredible peril.

8

Are Human Rights
the Moral Foundation of
American Foreign Policy?

"Human rights" is a phrase now so familiar to us and to most of the world that it is hard to believe that there is much about it still open to doubt. The phrase "human rights" has become so familiar not because hundreds of millions of people have suddenly taken to studying political philosophy but because it has become a central issue in foreign affairs. What used to be a doctrine for political philosophers to analyze and write about has been transported from the pages of political philosophy to the front page in newspapers around the world.

As in many highly theoretical matters, it is not easy to be sure what is really at stake. But of one thing we can be certain. Men and women in many parts of the world are risking harassment, imprisonment, torture, and even death in the name of what are called human rights. Because of their courage and dedication, if for no other reason, we cannot take lightly this issue of human rights.

Human rights have become so important to U.S. foreign policy that they figure in such decisions as whether we grant normal trade relations with other countries, whether détente is strained or strengthened, whether we and the Soviets progress in strategic arms limitation talks, whether we sell arms to other nations, and a host of other foreign policy and military policy matters. Human rights are the subject of UN declarations and UN commissions; the United States has an assistant secretary of state for human rights; the Congress receives human rights reports annually on 100 or so nations; and scores of nations hold months-long conferences to discuss human rights.

Critics of this development deplore the emphasis on human rights. They say that a foreign policy based on human rights is too idealistic, too lofty, too moralistic, too impractical, too likely to produce inconsistent and undesirable results, and too disruptive of good relations among nations, which must be based on interests, not universal ideals or morality.

Supporters of the emphasis on human rights argue that the U.S. government is based on the principle of human rights and that we must stand up for morality in the world or we stand for nothing. We lose influence, they argue, when we neglect morality. Vietnam, Watergate, and international bribery scandals have sullied our reputation and weakened our ability to impress other nations favorably. It is time for us to restore our moral standing in the world, by words and by deeds. The campaign for human rights will help us regain respect and self-respect in an honest and worthy fashion.

Because these two positions, for and against the emphasis on human rights in foreign policy, are so directly opposed, it is hard to see how anyone can disagree with both—but I do.

Human Rights and Morality

Both sides are persuaded that the essential ingredient of a human rights policy is morality. Both sides agree that standing for human rights is above all else a moral position. They differ only in that one applauds what the other deplores. My disagreement with both is basic: I do not think human rights stem from a *moral* position. Protection of human rights rests on something other than morality.

In fact, it is not possible to understand the significance of human rights and their role in American political life and in the world until we see how human rights differ from morality. I know it sounds strange. I know that President Jimmy Carter spoke of human rights as wholly a matter of morality. But as you read on, I think you will realize that I am not really saying anything new but rather recalling familiar themes that are well-known, that may have been forgotten, but that are easily recaptured.

In the long procession of Western political thought, the doctrine of human rights is a fairly recent invention or discovery. The great classical philosophic works had little or nothing to say about the *rights* of men. They had much to say about *duties* but practically nothing about *rights*. The same can be said about the Bible and old theological writing; if I am not mistaken, they, too, are silent about human rights.

The ancients *were* very concerned about ethics and morality. For them the excellence of the people was the chief goal of government. The best political society was the one that formed the best human beings. Ancient political writing dealt with questions of who should rule (their answer: the best, not the richest or the most numerous) and with inquiries about the best way for men and women to spend their lives.

If the chief business of government is thought to be to make good men and women, one must know what human goodness is and how to nurture it in a variety of circumstances. So the study of the best society was inseparably connected to the study of human character, or ethics, and the study of good and evil, or morality. For them, thinking about *government* was inseparable from thinking about ethics and morality. Nevertheless, the ancients did not think about human *rights* when they thought about ethics and morality. They did think about human *duties*.

If the question was whether some person ought to be allowed to read some questionable political treatise, perhaps on the subject of the origins of political communities, the ancients would begin by asking how old the person was, whether he was a citizen or a slave, how well educated he was, how capable he was of understanding and not being misled by false doctrine, and—perhaps most important—what his *duties* were in the political community. They might very well have decided that such and such a person should be allowed to read a treatise that might be dangerous for others because his intelligence and his judgment were excellent and his responsibilities in the community required him to make decisions that would benefit from such reading and similar study. We behave in an analogous manner, for example, in the handling of secret or classified information. Judgments of who may read classified papers are judgments of intelligence, character, training, and "need to know." At their root is an assertion of "the national interest." In short, the *right* to read, for the ancients, would depend on one's *duties* as a citizen. In ancient thought rights are not primary; rights are derived from duties. Since such rights depend on circumstances, they are temporary and revocable and thus not truly rights.

It is important to remember that I am talking not about a different human nature but about a different doctrine. As we can see from poems and plays thousands of years old, men and women thought and acted differently then, no doubt, but not *much* differently—that is, not so differently that we are unable to understand the behavior of Odysseus or Oedipus or Antigone, or the arguments of Socrates. Just because writers on political subjects did not speak of human rights does not mean that the conflicts between *private* interests and *public* interests did not exist.

The ancients dealt extensively with that great problem. The question was then, as it is now, how to lead citizens to put the good of the community as a whole ahead of their own private advantage whenever there is a conflict. The inclination to look out for one's self first does not come from reading books about the primacy of the individual; it is a human tendency that develops without instruction; ancient thinkers, too, were concerned to bring that tendency under control.

Some remedy is essential, and what often happens in practice is that force is used to make citizens act for the public good by punishing any disobedience severely. As a simple example, farmers can be *forced* to hand over more of their crop than they would like to hand over, keeping much less than they would like to keep for themselves and their own families, to feed fellow citizens in a time of need or for some other public reason.

If the same goal can be achieved without force, by inculcating in farmers and others a civic spirit of sacrifice and devotion to the whole community so that they willingly contribute to the public supply of food, proudly providing voluntary service to their country, that is certainly more desirable than using force. This can be done and is done by education, or by indoctrination, or by a regimented way of life, or by persuading the people that the monarch rules by divine right, or sometimes even through stories—whether true or not—of the divine origins of the community.

Complete success, of course, would mean that citizens—some, at least, if not all—would see no conflict; they would be convinced that they were doing what was best for themselves by doing what was best for the political community. For example, the aim of the educational system set forth in Plato's *Republic* is to ensure that citizens in every group or class or level of the republic see their own happiness as inseparable from the well-being of the community. But even in that imagined political community, some, if not all, had to be persuaded by myths and lies—noble lies but lies nevertheless—that citizens were profoundly unequal, some fit to rule and others fit to obey, even though all were born fellow citizens.

My main point in reminding you of ancient writers is to emphasize that although they had a deep concern with morality, they did not write about human rights. Morality and human rights are not necessarily linked.

The turning point in political philosophy came about 500 years ago and was expressed succinctly by Machiavelli. He said that others had imagined political societies but because his intention was "to write something useful," it was important not to confuse "what is done and what should be done." Machiavelli warned that any political leader who forgets or disregards the "great gap between how men live and how men ought to live" exposes himself to mortal danger.

By the time John Locke was writing, at the end of the seventeenth century, the unquestioned starting point for thinking about political society was human beings as they are, not as they ought to be. When Plato spoke of human nature, he meant what human beings could become through a life devoted to inquiry, the completion and perfection of what a human being ought to be. When Locke spoke of human nature, he meant what human beings are without benefit of civilizing or education—in terms of powerful desires, like the desire for self-preservation.

The political teaching that guided the founders of the American republic was—not in all respects but definitely in this one respect—almost completely a reversal of the ancient teaching: Men and women are not born citizens, are not citizens by nature; they are equal, not unequal; and they are born free. They start with rights. Every human being, we say, is *born* with rights. Those rights are ours by nature, by human nature; they are so much a part of us that they not only cannot be taken away legitimately, we are unable to consent voluntarily to give them away. That is what is meant by calling rights "unalienable."

That word "unalienable"—brings me to the end of this brief, incomplete, unavoidable lesson in the history of political philosophy. The Declaration of Independence speaks of unalienable rights, and the Declaration of Independence is *our* founding document. It explains what we mean when we speak of human rights, and it is what men and women all over the world who long for freedom think of first when they speak of human rights.

The United States was the first nation in the world to found itself explicitly on the principle of human rights. Our founding principle is that we are all endowed, equally, with rights to life and liberty. More, those rights are so important and fundamental that they are what government is all about: "Governments are instituted among men . . . to secure those rights."

It is important to be clear that we Americans assert *more* than that human beings have rights. We assert that the great reason for the existence of government is to protect those rights. Securing rights is the chief business of government; that task determines its character, its scope, and its limitations.

Limited Government

Limited government is not always seen as the inescapable consequence of the doctrine of human rights. Hobbes, for one, based his absolute monarchy on natural rights. The great problem is that government must be strong *enough* to protect rights without being *so* strong that it deprives the people of their rights. Is it possible to draw and maintain such a fine line? Can we make government strong enough to secure our rights to life and liberty from foes domestic and foreign without producing a government so strong that it tyrannizes over us and deprives us of our rights, as has happened down through history and has been the usual fate of men and women in much of the world all through this century, right down to the present moment?

The profoundly American answer to this question is to be found in *The Federalist*, but it is also to be found in the heads of Americans and in their very bones. In fact, what James Madison wrote in *The Federalist* in 1788, just after the Constitution was written and just before it was ratified, was an explanation of "the interior structure of the government," "the principles and structure of the government" provided by the proposed Constitution.

Because that Constitution *was* adopted, because that government did come into existence, and because we have lived under it for 200 years, we Americans have been formed by it. It has influenced our thinking about ourselves and human beings everywhere and, as often happens, has influenced us much more than we are always aware, so that sometimes we are brought up short, surprised by some foreigner saying, "Oh sure, that's the way you see it; that's the way you Americans think." There are some views almost all Americans share because of the way we are constituted as a nation and a people.

Madison stated the question directly and briefly: "In framing a government, . . . the great difficulty lies in this: you must first enable the government to control the governed; and in the next place oblige it to control itself."

It is beyond my purpose here to follow in detail Madison's discussion of the separation of powers and the importance of placing them in separate hands. What is to the point is to follow what he says about how such separation of powers limits the powers of the government to tyrannize over us and how the limits can be maintained. He does not advise us to rely on the morality or self-restraint or public-spiritedness of those in authority. He talks instead about the ambitions and interests of officeholders, about their strong personal interests. Power placed in the hands of many ambitious persons, in different parts of the government, will be used to keep "each other in their proper places," and that, he says, is "essential to the preservation of liberty."

The most important defense against a concentration of power in one person or one part of the government, Madison says, "consists in

giving to those who administer each department the necessary constitutional means and *personal motives* to resist encroachments of the
others. . . . Ambition must be made to counteract ambition. The
interest of the man must be connected with the constitutional rights of
the place."

Consider how much this differs from the efforts of the ancients to
subordinate private or selfish advantage to the public good. Here,
Madison tells us, the desire for personal, selfish advantage is not only
something to tolerate, it is a force to be put to work for the public
good, for the protection of liberty, for the protection of the rights of
citizens. What will keep in check the ambition for dangerous power of
officeholders? The counteracting ambition of other officeholders.
Should we try to get rid of ambitious power-seeking persons in office?
Only if we can be sure to get rid of *all* of them, in *all* parts of the
government. If we have ambitious men and women in one branch, or
even one unusually skillful and ambitious person in one branch, and
none in the others, who will "counteract" that ambition? Without such
counteraction, power might be concentrated and the rights of citizens
endangered.

Madison does not rely on discipline or education or religion or
any form of good motives to control government officials. He calls the
constitutional system a "policy of supplying, by opposite and rival
interests, the *defect* of better motives." By this policy, "the private
interest of every individual may be a sentinel over the public rights."

Madison carries his analysis several steps beyond. In this country the "power surrendered by the people is first divided," because we
also have state governments, and federal power is further divided into
the three branches. "Hence a double security arises to the rights of the
people. The different governments will control each other, at the same
time that each will be controlled by itself."

Multiplicity of Interests

Even these precautions are not enough, according to Madison. Government is not the only danger to the rights of citizens; we must also
"guard one part of the society against the injustice of the other part."
Here his concern is that a persisting majority will become an unjust
and tyrannical majority and will violate the rights of the minority. The
protection he calls for is to make sure that the society is large enough
and varied enough to include very many groups and interests. Under
the extended republic established by the Constitution, "the society
itself will be broken into so many parts, interests, and classes of

citizens, that the rights of individuals . . . will be in little danger from interested combinations of the majority."

To see the relevance of all this to human rights policy, I suggest that we try a little Madisonian reasoning about rights. If someone asked *us* today what security there is for religious rights in this country, *we* would answer, would we not, that our *first* line of defense is the First Amendment. Madison's answer in *The Federalist* is somewhat different: the *first* line of defense of religious rights is the multiplicity of religious sects. He gives the same answer to the question of what protects civil rights: "In a free government the security for civil rights must be the same as that for religious rights. It consists in the one case in the multiplicity of interests, and in the other in the multiplicity of sects. The degree of security [of rights] in both cases will depend on the number of interests and sects." The implication is that if there were few sects or if one sect were a persistent majority, religious rights would be in danger no matter what the Constitution might say.

Madison subsequently played the leading role in the adoption of the First Amendment, and that amendment now provides a powerful defense of religious rights. But it can also be argued that the continuing multiplicity of religious sects is simultaneously a basic support and one of the most important consequences of the First Amendment.

Earlier I said that morality and human rights were not necessarily linked for the ancients. The same assertion can be made for Madison. By this look at the argument of Madison on protective rights, we see that the notion of making rights the basis of government begins by turning *away* from the ancient task of reforming men and women in some fashion, seeking to make them virtuous, and turning *toward* harnessing the great forces of *private* interest and ambition.

A government that can be *relied* on to respect the rights of individuals must be designed with great care in its principles and its institutions. Rights-respecting nations need not be just like the United States. But if Madison is right, they must have many parts, which must be rivals of one another in significant respects, and they must have ambitious persons in positions of power whose personal interests and ambitions lead them to fight for their constitutional rights. In addition, the people must be numerous and must have varied and competing interests. *Then* rights have a fighting chance.

How would Madison respond if we asked him to estimate the safety of the rights of individuals in a nation lacking such a constitution, government, and society; where there is a great concentration of power in the hands of one person or one party; where there is no opposition press; where there is only one employer or, if more, where property and enterprises can be confiscated with impunity; where there are no labor unions or no free ones; and where the society is not varied and the interests not free to organize? How effective would he think exhortation in the name of human rights might be? He surely would not be confident that such efforts would produce happy results. He would warn that pledges "delineated on paper" without the "auxiliary precautions" he described are a mere "parchment barrier," very easy to rip through. Depending on the "better motives" of those in power is not prudent. Words in the Constitution alone cannot protect rights; they must be buttressed by the way we are constituted as a people, as a series of governments, as a society with incredibly varied interest groups and with a multiplicity of religious sects.

The protection of rights in this country and in other countries similar to ours does not rely *primarily* on the good will, generosity, morality, or restraint of officials, although those desirable characteristics may be present. It does depend primarily on divisions and distributions of powers, diversity within the society, an enterprising competing spirit of the people, and established institutions, accommodations, and traditional practices.

Is it any wonder that dictators and leaders of Communist countries are amused at first when we speak to them about human rights and dismayed when they realize that we are serious and will take serious steps—like reducing trade or cutting off arms sales—in the name of human rights? We think we are asking them only for relatively simple steps—releasing some prisoners held for political reasons without having been charged or tried for committing a crime, allowing families to be reunited who have been kept apart by restrictions on emigration, or allowing their citizens freedom to read some foreign newspapers—and we find it hard to believe that others will see such commonplace decencies as disruptive or subversive.

When the heads of these tyrannical regimes realize how seriously we take this matter, they sense that what we are proposing is possible only by a profound alteration of their governments and perhaps also of their societies. In that way we democratic peoples are a threat to them, to their power, to their doctrines, and to their political legitimacy, just as in 1776 we were a threat to every absolute monarch claiming to rule by divine right, when we declared ourselves a nation in the name of individual rights.

Our differences with other regimes, profound as they are, are not best understood as *moral* differences, although they do have to do with character and constitution. Calling them moral differences misses the point. They are differences of a different sort, having to do with the nature of man, the purposes of government, and the limits of political power. Starting from the base of human rights, for example, it seems the most natural thing in the world to say that some things are just none of the government's business. Totalitarian doctrines differ completely; they are called totalitarian because they assert that their goals can be reached only if the powers of government extend to the *totality* of human thought and action. To reach that far into the lives and thoughts of citizens, to suppress all private, unauthorized activity, they must have unlimited powers. These unlimited powers are typically justified by some grand goal or vision of the distant future, when human nature will be transformed, all enemies will be eradicated, and harmony will prevail among all men, without the need of government.

Our Founding Principles

Many Americans wish that our own political principles were more lofty and visionary. They are disappointed in acknowledging that we have no utopian aspirations and that our goals cannot be stated in millennial terms, as Marxist and other ideological political doctrines can. But we need not be without consolation.

We ought to be willing to face up to the sober character of our nation and explain ourselves to ourselves and to the world in the light of our founding principles. Straight talk about what we are could have helpful consequences for us, for the world, and for oppressed peoples everywhere.

First, it makes us less self-righteous and makes us seem less self-righteous if we acknowledge that we are not angels. Our principles may be just, but we must not make the self-righteous mistake of confusing ourselves with our principles. We do often act unjustly. Providing security for human rights is not and has not been an easy task for us, although we have been at it for 200 years, with a constitutional government designed, above all else, for that purpose. Let us acknowledge that it is hard for us and harder for others, whose governments and societies have grown up under other doctrines and circumstances.

Consider that we have a Constitution based on Madison's principles. We have a large society with a bewildering multiplicity of interests. We have a system of separation of powers, and we have the "double security" of a federal system. The framers of the Constitution thought that all of that would suffice, but just to be sure, after their work was completed, the Bill of Rights was added. Even so, with all these protections for human rights, the history of the United States tells of 200 years of repeated and persistent violations of the rights of individuals and groups. The best we can say for ourselves is that in this country the law, the courts, the society, the Constitution, and public sentiment are all on the side of protecting rights.

We have progressed, perhaps, but who will claim that we can be satisfied that human rights violations are a thing of the past in the United States? No one, I hope. The problem of the danger to the rights of persons and groups is not one susceptible to a final solution.

Second, because men and women are not angels, let us emphasize that we do not think we can or should try to eradicate all evil in the world. That effort was explicit in nazism—in a distorted and grotesque form—and is implicit in Marxism-Leninism, in the expectation of reaching the classless society. We have seen that human suffering, misery, imprisonment, torture, and the slaughter of tens of millions of human beings can result from the combination of great military and police power and the willingness to use it to eradicate all supposed evil. Eradicating all evil—a "final solution" of central problems—most often takes the form of liquidating, that is, murdering, all those human beings who are thought to be the source of it. In the nuclear age we need not minimize our devotion to the cause of human rights, but we should make clear that we know that there is no final solution to the problem of human rights and that whatever power is mustered to protect rights must be used in moderation, with restraint, under law, through constitutional institutions.

Third, it helps in dealing with sovereign nations if one is not and does not sound "preachy." What we should avoid is sounding as if we think we are more moral, more angelic, than others—except as our character and behavior have been formed by 200 years under a rights-protecting Constitution.

We should explain that as we understand human rights—and we have long experience—no great moral demands need to be faced. It is more a matter of arrangements of institutions and interests than of moral uplift. The changes that are necessary, if Madison was correct, are massive and threatening to any tyranny, no doubt, but the need to think about tyranny in its many forms as it exists almost all over the world and about the necessary conditions for protection of rights is what we ought to be talking about in international forums, not who is more moral.

Finally, it is always good for us Americans to have sobering thoughts, to counteract our tendency to overoptimism and exuberance. The sobering thought I would prescribe is that good results do often come from questionable sources in this world, just as profoundly evil consequences, on a massive scale, have often come from

85

seemingly lofty and grand motives—I mean such things as Hitler's efforts to impose universal peace on the world by subjugating all mankind, whatever the cost in lives, suffering, and degradation.

Our American founding constitutional principles were a deliberate *turning away* from the use of government's power to achieve stated ethical and moral goals. This government means to leave to the nongovernmental sphere any effort to shape and mold human beings according to moral principles. Our founding principles were a *turning toward* acknowledging the strength and persistence of self-interest and the use of intellect and ingenuity to turn these to the service of the public interest. It should please moral men and women, nevertheless, that this world is so skillfully constituted that good results can be brought forth from imperfect and not very lofty human aspirations. They have produced, in the United States, in my opinion, a morally satisfying regime, especially when compared with other existing regimes rather than with some that have been imagined or hoped for.

One title the White House attached to the major foreign policy speech President Carter gave at Notre Dame University on human rights was "America's Goal: A Foreign Policy Based on Moral Values." What I think of that misguided aspiration is clear. Not only was he wrong in what he did say, he was even more wrong in what he failed to say. That important presidential pronouncement on the subject of human rights contained not a single reference to the Constitution of the United States.

9
Three Human Rights Are Enough

The cause of human rights has enemies in the world, bloody-minded and bloody-handed enemies who persecute, kidnap, torture, maim, and kill their victims, most of whom have committed no crime greater than trying to exercise the natural rights of free men and women to live a productive, inoffensive, decent life.

The fact that oppression is widespread and that there are killers in positions of power in much of the world, though obvious, is yet the necessary starting point for entering the American debate over human rights policy, because sometimes the heat of disagreement becomes so intense that we forget that ours is usually a dispute among partisans of liberty, not among enemies of liberty. As Thomas Jefferson said in his first Inaugural Address, "every difference of opinion is not a difference of principle." In these disputes, the question is not who loves human rights more but who knows how to defend them successfully. In judging a lawyer or a general, most of us are not content to be told that he is always wholeheartedly on the side of those he represents or leads; we also want to know whether he wins.

When we look at the human rights situation throughout the world, we must admit it is a dismal one, with few bright spots or signs of improvement, despite worldwide efforts by governments, the private sector, research institutes, international organizations, and a flood of publications. The efforts are, for the most part, ineffectual; the policy approach is wrong, or our understanding is faulty—or both.

It is important that human rights vigilance be maintained at a high level, because the suffering of innocent victims is immense and we should try to rescue as many as we can. Less urgent but more important are efforts for improving our understanding, which I offer in the name and for the advancement of the cause of human rights.

Basic Rights

I will begin with basics. We must all breathe, eat, drink, and work to live, and we must do these in a certain way in order to live well.

87

Spokesmen of the human rights movement consider it important to name these necessities as rights and propose, write down, and ratify as human rights clean air, an adequate diet, unpolluted water, and a job. These rights are included in many international documents and are not included in the old American documents such as state constitutions and the Constitution of the United States. Spokesmen of the human rights movement strongly advocate American support for adoption of these rights and many more, perhaps for ourselves but certainly for the rest of the world.

Surely there is no dispute among thoughtful Americans that we all have the right to life and the means necessary to sustain it. That is the starting point of all natural rights teaching, beginning more than three hundred years ago in the writings of Thomas Hobbes and John Locke. That right is asserted in the Declaration of Independence and is so taken for granted in the Constitution as a basic truth that it is not spoken of in the body of the Constitution as initially ratified but only referred to in the Fifth Amendment: "No person shall . . . be deprived of life, liberty, or property without due process of law." The question, then, is, Do we strengthen or weaken the protection of the right to life and liberty by adding to legal documents a list of the necessary supports of life? Two dangers are immediately apparent in the codification of such rights: first, it can give a false sense that asserting the right addresses the problem of obtaining food, water, air, and work; second, it can lead to an increase in the power of government agencies in new and unwelcome ways.

Declaring the right to an adequate diet does not augment the supply of food or improve its distribution. If we think of the plight of desperate peoples, with hundreds of thousands dying of malnutrition, can it help to insist that these people have a right to an adequate diet? The question is not whether they have the right, but how to get food to them, how to correct the problems that led to the lack of food, and how to put their agricultural production on a sounder footing. Surely no one seriously asserts that a significant part of the problem of hunger in the world stems from a denial that people have the right to an adequate diet.

It distresses me, thinking of the plight of the hungry millions in the world, most of them victims of misconceived government policies more than of natural deficiencies, that their well-fed diplomatic representatives in international organizations devote so much time and money to creating the cruel illusion that asserting the right in some international document will somehow provide more food for the hungry. It is either a conscious fraud or a naive faith in the magic of words to assert that recognizing the human right to enough food will resolve the problem. Whether fraud or folly, it is deplorable and shameful.

Guaranteeing Rights

There is another danger in asserting these life-supporting rights. If we had in our Constitution, as some nations do, a guaranteed right to an adequate diet, to adequate shelter at a reasonable rent, to a job, and to other things, how would the government honor these guarantees? I am talking about taking the guarantees *seriously,* as something the government is pledged and *obliged* to do. When unemployment rises, it will not suffice just to increase appropriations for unemployment insurance. It will be necessary for the government to generate jobs, either on the public payroll or by controlling industry. Most other Western nations not having completely controlled economies but having more government-owned and government-controlled industry than in the United States have been unable to diminish unemployment any more successfully than the United States has during recessions.

Figures for the Soviet Union and other state-controlled economies are hard to come by, but it is known that they have low unemployment, a great deal of underemployment, low wages, and major subsidy by the entire population to keep job levels higher by sustaining uneconomic enterprise. That method is used for minimizing unemployment, but it can be carried further where the government is the sole employer and investor. Where the state guarantees the right to a job and takes it seriously, it is hard to see how it can stop short of controlling the entire economy—the training and placement of workers, the allocation of resources for investment, the opening and closing of workplaces.

If the U.S. Constitution included a guarantee of the right to a job, what would the federal government do? Neither Congress nor the president has the power to honor such a guarantee. It is common for Americans to speak of the constitutional guarantees of rights, but as a matter of fact none are guaranteed. Our First Amendment rights, for example, are spoken of as preexisting; the security they have is that "Congress shall make no law" to abridge or prohibit their exercise. The formulation is negative, a restraint on the power of government. The positive formulation found in other constitutions and advocated by human rights spokesmen, in which the government guarantees a long list of rights, *adds* to the power of government, authorizing it to act in an area forbidden by our Bill of Rights. If the state guarantees freedom of the press, the first action, typically, is to establish a government agency to supervise the press to ensure that it remains "free" in its daily operations.

The strategy of the U.S. Constitution with regard to rights is to rely on denials of government power and to avoid the ascendancy of such power over rights. The word "guarantee" does not occur anywhere in the Constitution in regard to rights but only in the aptly named guarantee clause: "The United States shall guarantee to every State in this Union a Republican form of government." That, by the way, is a sound way—and certainly a brief one—to secure rights.

There is a real danger in enumerating rights, especially if the list is long and affirmative and guaranteed. If one guarantees education, housing, and jobs, for instance, the state will end up being the only schoolmaster, landlord, and boss; extend the guaranteed rights to health care, resorts, retirement pensions, and such, as is done in many constitutions, and it is easy to see that the government, if it takes these guarantees seriously, must control almost the totality of activities—another way of saying it must be totalitarian. Rights are most secure where the constitutional list is short, negative, and free of guarantees.

What Is a Bill of Rights?

The cause of human rights would be greatly strengthened if we understood better what a bill of rights is. The U.S. Bill of Rights is a set of ten amendments to the Constitution; the human rights provisions in the United Nations Charter are in the preamble and three articles. Each is part of a document that establishes institutions and assigns and limits responsibilities and powers. Americans often speak of the Bill of Rights as if *it* were the Constitution. The Bill of Rights, extraordinary achievement that it is, would be almost useless in a badly constituted political society. This is not a speculative statement; there are nations in whose constituting documents the U.S. provisions have been copied almost verbatim but where they have no effect. James Madison believed that protection for freedom of religion, for instance, in the Constitution would be useless, a "paper barrier," if members of any one religious sect were in the majority.

We have preserved as much religious liberty as we have in this nation (and it is always being tested and always in jeopardy) through a combination of the prohibition against an established church, encouragement of religious freedom, and the existence of a multiplicity of religious sects. These interact and tend to support each other. If any one were absent, the situation would be different. Without the multiplicity of religious sects, nothing in political experience would make us expect religious freedom to survive, no matter what it says in the First Amendment. Rights prosper in societies constituted to encourage and support them; they cannot survive through the power of words on parchment, unless one believes in the magical power of incantation.

The Constitution of the United States drafted by the framers, analyzed and praised in *The Federalist* for the security it provided for our rights, and ratified by the states was the Constitution without the Bill of Rights. When a public cry arose during the ratification process for the addition of a bill of rights, Madison and Alexander Hamilton opposed it as unwise and unnecessary, because they were convinced that enumerating rights held certain dangers and, further, that the Constitution already secured rights effectively by constituting the nation in a way that encouraged the exercise of rights and discouraged government abridgment or violation of them. As Hamilton wrote, "The truth is, after all the declamations we have heard, that the Constitution is itself, in every rational sense, and to every useful purpose, A BILL OF RIGHTS." And this was said of a constitution in which the word "right" occurs only once, in reference to "the exclusive right" of authors and inventors to their works, hardly a natural right

Madison, as a representative from Virginia in the first Congress, became the initial author of the Bill of Rights. In doing so he sought to design a bill of rights not subject to his objections to bills of rights. The opponents of the Constitution were attempting to convene a new constitutional convention, and much of their support was coming from supporters of the Constitution who wanted explicit protection of rights. By proposing his amendments, Madison ended the threat of a new convention. But the amendments he proposed were designed to change the original Constitution as little as possible. Once they were ratified, they were little used for decades (for more than a century, in fact), primarily because the Constitution did its work of constituting the nation in a structure that gives rights their best chance. When the amendments were ratified, both advocates and critics agreed that ratification changed almost nothing. That was not because these provisions were inconsequential; it was because they added to but did not alter a constitution that was working well. But now we take the body of the Constitution too much for granted and speak about the Bill of Rights as if it were the Constitution itself. Harm is done thereby, but not as much as if the institutional arrangements established by the Constitution were not in place, functioning and jealously guarded.

It is otherwise in human rights foreign policy and the policy of international organizations. There great harm is done by talking about

91

declarations of rights as if they were self-sufficient and self-activating, which they are not. It is but another example of a curious faith in the magical powers of words, a false reliance that distracts our attention from the real dangers and the real remedies and can only add frustration, disappointment, and bitterness to the suffering we seek to diminish.

The Dark Side of Human Rights

This leads me to my final difficulty with the arguments of human rights spokesmen. They seem to ignore what might be called the dark side of human rights. It is not true that human rights teachings come from our religious heritage; if I am not mistaken, no place in the Bible speaks of rights. The reader of the Bible is instructed in duties, not rights. Thomas Jefferson knew that it was not necessary to connect religion and rights; he was able to speak of the self-evident truth of the equality of men in their rights without referring to a divine source. The prayerful phrases in the Declaration of Independence— "endowed by their Creator," "appealing to the Supreme Judge of the world," and "with a firm reliance on the Protection of Divine Providence"—were not in Jefferson's original draft but were added subsequently, in the Committee of Five and in the Continental Congress.

There is also reason to doubt the necessary connection of rights and morality. The authors of the great works of classical political philosophy wrote lengthy and profound works on the subject of justice but never wrote about natural rights. Locke, however, based his teachings about the origin, extent, and end of civil society on the primacy of rights. His other works—on philosophy, psychology, economics, theology, and education—abound in discussions of morality. In his book on politics the word "morality"—or anything like it—does not occur. Locke's book, the great source of political liberty for the American founders, is the first significant writing to set forth a comprehensive account of political society that does not include a discussion of justice. Natural rights displaced the word "justice."

Human rights, or natural rights, derive from the powerful human desire for self-preservation. It is self-evident that we have a right to do what we can to preserve ourselves, because we *know* we have a right to life. We have a right, therefore, to actions that defend our life—a right to liberty. We have also a right to those things necessary to sustain and nourish ourselves—a right to property. Our awareness of these rights is strong and natural and requires no instruction. But the exercise of these rights leads to difficulties, because we come into conflict and competition with others as we exercise our rights. It becomes clear, to some at least, that the ability to enjoy my rights depends to a great extent on protecting your rights and the rights of all others. That consequence of natural rights requires instruction and much more than instruction; it requires commands, rules, judgment, and enforcement. What comes naturally does not suffice; we must learn, as Locke put it, that "where there is no law, there is no freedom"—and that has not been an easy or natural lesson for mankind.

To make it easier to accept this unnatural outcome of natural rights teaching, we acknowledge powers exerted over us as legitimate, as political rather than dictatorial, only if those powers derive from our own consent. Some things, it is assumed, we will not consent to. That is the meaning of the opening words of our Bill of Rights: even if a majority of the people and a majority of Congress want to abridge the freedom of speech or prohibit the free exercise of religion, Congress shall make no such law. If the government uses its power to prohibit the free exercise of religion, that is not political power but dictatorial power, not legitimized by the Constitution—not "just powers" derived "from the consent of the governed."

There is a natural human tendency to violate the rights of others in the pursuit of one's own rights and interests. We see it frequently in this country—individuals against individuals, groups against groups. Much of the history of the United States can be told by recounting the efforts of certain groups—in the legislatures, the courts, the executive agencies, and the private sector—to exercise their own rights more effectively by curtailing the rights of others.

In extolling the importance of human rights, we must realize that they stem from a political teaching based on strife and harsh competition, with pain, suffering, deprivation, and misery often resulting. A nation whose political scheme is based on the primacy of individual rights is one of confusion, turmoil, and ferment—and, unavoidably, not a little injustice. It is not a design for calm and harmony in national life. It is a design for a stormy, tumultuous, and chaotic peace, but one we can consent to.

Most human beings, after all, have never known government they would or could consent to. Their choice is to resist or submit. In such societies human rights have no standing, no matter what the rhetoric. If one is given a fair trial or is interrogated without torture or is allowed to emigrate, it is not a matter of right but only of policy, a gift or privilege bestowed by the state. That is why so much of the effort of human rights activists has no effect or a very brief one.

Some think it sullies the ideals of political liberty and human rights to acknowledge their dark and lowly origins, but this is a shallow view. It is one of the greatest ironies of the human condition

93

that despicable tyrannies—Khomeini's Iran being only the most recent example—are often born of lofty ideals—like the love of God—which then become corrupted, twisted, and unrecognizable; and that modernity's greatest political achievement, a government of sustained, ordered liberty, an inspiration to humankind for centuries, is born of the basic human desire for self-preservation and the fierce determination—natural in us all—to look out for ourselves.

That independence, we have found, can be nurtured as well as governed under a skillfully constituted government and, at the same time, can be shaped and expanded to inculcate in the citizenry a loving concern for the well-being and freedom of others. We can be prouder of the system of liberty and better able to expand and continue it if we understand its lowly origin. It is not unknown in nature for ugly parents to give birth to a beautiful child.

Conclusion

What then can be said about the insistent call for an emphasis on human rights in our foreign policy? We can say that the demand for long lists of new economic and social rights is probably misguided and will probably do more harm than good, that the emphasis on declarations of rights rather than on constitutions means focusing on the appendage rather than the core of the problem. We can say that we would do better in understanding what human rights are and how we can best secure them, for ourselves and for the billions denied them, if we understood better what natural rights are and where they come from.

What can we do to improve the world? We can look more closely at our own scheme for securing rights and at the skills that have protected them. Our Constitution acknowledges the human rights of life, liberty, and property, and the political rights of free speech, free press, freedom of religion, assembly, petition, habeas corpus, public trial, and legal counsel; it prohibits self-incrimination, cruel and unusual punishments, ex post facto laws, and bills of attainder; and it establishes an independent judiciary. How many ills of the world, how many sins against human rights would we not eradicate if these protections for rights were established and enforced around the world?

This is the starting point for a program for human rights. It may not be enough, but let us do that much first. If that is too much to do or to hope for, why, then, spend our time trying to think of new formulations of human rights in addition to the ones we know? If the complaint is that I propose too much, would that not suggest that the more extended program proposed by many human rights advocates is not meant seriously as an undertaking of actions but only of words, not for the sake of the improvement of the lot of the miserable of the world, but for other, unstated reasons?

President Jefferson was surely right that not every difference of opinion is a difference of principle, but it is as surely right that some differences of opinion are, indeed, differences of principle.

PART THREE

Political Philosophy—
The Key to Locke

10
A Reading of Locke's Chapter "Of Property"

The excellent chapter on property . . . would be sufficient, if all Locke's other writings had perished, to leave him a high name in philosophy.

HENRY HALLAM[1]

In his *Two Treatises of Government*, John Locke begins "Of Property" with a promise to show his readers how private property originated.

> . . . 'tis very clear that God . . . has given the earth to the children of men, given it to mankind in common. But this being supposed, it seems to some a very great difficulty how anyone should ever come to have a property in anything. . . . I shall endeavor to show how men might come to have a property in several parts of that which God gave to mankind in common, and that without any express compact of all the commoners [§25].[2]

In the original universal common of which Locke speaks, "nobody has originally a private dominion exclusive of the rest of mankind" (§26). Every man has an equal right to every part of what is common. This cannot mean, however, that everyone has a share in the ownership of everything; it can only mean that originally there was no ownership, there was no property. If in the universal common any man has a right to help himself to any part of the common without the consent of the others, then the others have no property, for it is the nature of property "that without a man's own consent, it cannot be taken from him" (§193). The assertion that the world was given to mankind in common means simply that in the beginning no one owned anything. The original universal common was a state of universal propertylessness. That is why Locke proceeds at once to the question: How did anyone "ever come to have a property in anything"?

The answer lies in this, that there was one exception to the otherwise universal common; that sole exception was the person of each man himself:

> Though the earth and all inferior creatures be common to all men, yet every man has a property in his own person. This nobody has any right to but himself [§27].

Furthermore, every man owns not only his own person but also his own labor, which is the immediate extension of his person: "the labor of his body and the work of his hands, we may say, are properly his" (§27). The property that every man has in his own person and in his own labor is the original and natural property; it is the foundation of all other property in the state of nature. All other property, then, was derivative from that original, natural, and underived property.

In the earliest times there were vast uncultivated territories and very few men; there were therefore ample supplies of natural provisions fit for food—fruits and wild beasts. In this setting of abundance (and even superabundance) of provisions, the apples you gathered were yours, for you had combined what belonged only to you (your labor in gathering them) with something that belonged to no one (the apples hanging on the trees or lying on the ground). Someone else might contest your property in them, claiming that, by removing those apples from the common state, you had deprived him of the opportunity to take them for himself. Although this objection would otherwise be valid, it is fully overcome by a reminder of the condition of abundance, in the form of a decisive and always present qualification: whatever you remove from the natural common and mix your labor with is yours *where there is enough and as good left in common for others*" (§27, italics added). In the universal common you come to own unowned apples simply by picking them, if there are so many more unowned apples left on and under the trees that anyone else may have as many simply by picking them himself. Another who contests your property in the picked apples is really not claiming the apples that are common. If apples alone are all he wants, there are enough and as good still left for his taking. By claiming the apples already in your possession, he is really seeking only the labor you have mixed with them—and to that labor he never had any right:

> For this labor being the unquestionable property of the laborer, no man but he can have a right to what that is once joined to, at least where there is enough and as good left in common for others [§27].

Property in land is, in the original common, acquired in the same way. "As much land as a man tills, plants, improves, cultivates, and can use the product of, so much is his property" (§32). If the objection is raised that by thus enclosing the land he deprived another, the same rebuttal, based on the same qualification, applies:

> Nor was this appropriation of any parcel of land by improving it any prejudice to any other man, since there was still enough and as good left, and more than the yet unprovided could use. So that, in effect, there was never the less left for others because of his enclosure for himself. For he that leaves as much as another can make use of does as good as take nothing at all [§33].

This property is a combination of what is private, labor, and what is common, the land. Why then does the combination of the private and the common produce a result that is wholly private?

> Nor is it so strange, as perhaps before consideration it may appear, that the property of labor should be able to overbalance the community of land. For it is labor indeed that puts the difference of value on everything . . . [§40].

When there is so much land for so few people, however much one may enclose, more than enough remains for the others: it is as if nothing had been taken. What is taken is of little or no account; land without labor "would scarcely be worth anything" (§43). This is another way Locke has of stating why the combination of the private and the common results in private property: the private component, labor, constitutes almost entirely the value of the thing; the materials, the common element, are "scarce to be reckoned in." Labor gives title to property in the state of nature primarily because "labor makes the far greatest part of the value of things we enjoy in this world" (§42). If the addition of my labor made something valuable that was, without it, "almost worthless" (§43), then surely, my labor being the only thing of value in it, it must be acknowledged that the labor made it mine.

There are two reasons why the natural provisions are, in themselves, almost worthless. The first is that an apple can provide no benefit to a man until it is picked or in some way appropriated nor a deer until it is hunted and caught. The fruits and beasts, as they exist in nature before any addition of human effort, are useless to man. As an apple on another continent is of no use, so it is with an apple ten feet away until the addition of labor.

The second reason why the natural provisions are almost worthless is precisely their very great abundance, which would constitute a surplus supply when the number of human beings is relatively very small. In speaking of the provisions as worthless, Locke does not mean that they are unimportant for survival. The air we breathe and

POLITICAL PHILOSOPHY—THE KEY TO LOCKE

the water we drink are vital, but where air and water are superabundant we would not pay for a breath or a drink. The natural materials, like anything that is present in practically unlimited abundance, could not command a price or a barter equivalent. This seems to indicate that Locke had in mind some early form of the law of supply and demand; it should not surprise us, therefore, to find in his economic writings the statement that value or price is determined by "quantity and vent" (roughly equivalent to supply and demand) and "no other way in the world":

> He that will justly estimate the value of any thing, must consider its quantity in proportion to its vent, for this alone regulates the price. The value of any thing . . . is greater, as its quantity is less in proportion to its vent. . . . For if you alter the quantity, or vent, on either side, you presently alter the price, but no other way in the world.
> For it is not the being, adding, increasing, or diminishing of any good quality in any commodity, that makes its price greater or less; but only as it makes its quantity, or vent, greater or less, in proportion one to another.[3]

The original condition was an abundance of almost worthless provisions; it was not an actual plenty but only a potential plenty, to be made actual by human labor and invention. What seems at first to be a kind of paradise, a vast expanse of fertile land well stocked with "the fruits it naturally produces and beasts it feeds," all "produced by the spontaneous hand of nature" (§26), "the common mother of all" (§28), and with very "few spenders" (§31) to consume this abundance, is in fact a compound of too much of what is almost worthless and not enough of what is necessary to make it valuable—human labor. The general "penury" (§32) of the primitive state is comparable to the condition of the Indians, America's "needy and wretched inhabitants" (§37),

> who are rich in land and poor in all the comforts of life; whom nature having furnished as liberally as any other people with *the materials of plenty*, i.e., a fruitful soil, apt to produce in abundance what might serve for food, raiment, and delight, yet *for want of improving it by labor* have not one-hundredth part of the conveniences we enjoy [§41, italics added].

Another major cause of the penury of the original common is that "the greatest part of things really useful to the life of man . . . are generally things of short duration, such as, if they are not consumed by use, will decay and perish of themselves" (§46). This natural fact of spoiling was perhaps the major limitation of property in the state of nature.

Nature does severely limit property in the universal common: "As much as any one can make use of to any advantage of life before it spoils, so much he may by his labor fix a property in. Whatever is beyond this is more than his share and belongs to others" (§31). The possession of land was similarly limited:

> whatsoever he tilled and reaped, laid up and made use of before it spoiled, that was his peculiar right; whatsoever he enclosed and could feed and make use of, the cattle and product was also his. But if either the grass of his enclosure rotted on the ground or the fruit of his planting perished without gathering and laying up, this part of the earth, notwithstanding his enclosure, was still to be looked on as waste, and might be the possession of any other [§38].

Locke seems to have derived from the natural fact of spoiling a kind of rule to ensure the fair distribution of goods in the universal common. The reasoning is plausible, but consideration of two questions reveals the inadequacy of that interpretation of Locke's discussion of spoiling. First, why is such a rule necessary? Second, would it be effective?

The foundation of property in the original condition must be a superabundance of natural provisions. Your labor in picking an apple makes it your property if enough apples and as good are left for others. When there is such an abundance, what need is there for a rule to limit accumulation? The quantity you take can make no difference to me, as long as you leave me enough and as good; nor would I care whether what you have taken spoils or not in your possession. If you are so foolish as to waste your labor acquiring more than you can use, you cheat yourself, but you do not cheat me.

Some means of limiting accumulation is required only if there is less than a superabundance, only if what is taken leaves less than enough for others. Whether a rule based on spoiling would serve to limit accumulation even in that case depends on whether it is applied to perishable or durable goods. Suppose that a man achieves an effective local monopoly of nuts, leaving not one for others; since they might "last good for his eating a whole year" (§46), he could take that long to eat his way through his supply without any spoiling. The spoiling rule would be ineffective in limiting possession of these scarce, durable goods. It would not achieve a fair distribution of them.

Any rule limiting accumulation is unnecessary when there is a very great plenty of provisions. If, under other conditions, such a rule is necessary, one based on spoiling is ineffective for durable goods. The spoiling rule can be necessary *and* effective as a means toward fair sharing only when there is a scarcity of perishable goods. But the establishment of property in the original condition, by mixing labor with the natural provisions, depends entirely on a very great abundance, one that automatically achieves the leaving of enough for others. If there is not enough for everyone, not even labor can establish a right to a part of the whole to the exclusion of all other men. If labor cannot establish a title to property when there is a scarcity, then nothing can. There is no other way in the original state. Title may be transferred by barter or purchase, but only labor can *begin* property. In short, if there is a scarcity of perishable provisions in the original state, there cannot be natural property. There can be only possession of what is common. The conclusion is that even when the scarce perishable thing is in your possession, any other man still has as good a claim to it as you have. In the struggle for possession that would ensue, right would be established by the might of the stronger, and it would be difficult, if not impossible, to keep more for yourself than could be quickly consumed.

The fact of spoiling does indeed limit possessions in the original state and keep every man in a state of penury. "Nothing was made by God for man to spoil or destroy" (§31), we are told, but if all the denizens of the original universal common had become so demented as to devote their entire labor to spoiling as much as they could, the results of their combined efforts would be as nothing compared with the extensive spoiling and waste occurring throughout the vast territory "left to nature" (§37). When we consider "the plenty of natural provisions there was a long time in the world, and the few spenders" (§31), the spoiling that could not be blamed on man is appalling. The spoiling of things by the hand of man is dwarfed by the spoiling that occurs beyond his reach. Natural spoiling can be lessened only by an alteration of the prevailing conditions.

However much Locke deplored wastefulness and destruction, his discussion of spoiling does not point toward a moral rule of fair dealing with other men in the original state. It indicates, rather, the massive scale of waste under the rule of nature; it points toward the necessity of discovering some means of liberation from that harsh rule.

The third factor contributing to the penury of the earliest stage of the universal common is the lack of cultivation of the land: "land that is left wholly to nature . . . is called, as indeed it is, *waste*" (§42); the extent of this natural waste can be lessened, therefore, by the spread of agriculture. One is mistaken to think that a man deprives others by enclosing land to cultivate it for his own use. Because cultivated land is much more productive than uncultivated land, all his neighbors will benefit:

> . . . I have heard it affirmed that in Spain itself a man may be permitted to plough, sow, and reap, without being disturbed, upon land he has no other title to but only his making use of it. . . . The inhabitants think themselves beholden to him who by his industry on neglected and, consequently, waste land has increased the stock of corn which they wanted [§36].

Agriculture then is a major step toward alleviating the penury of man's original condition, but its effectiveness is limited by the fact of spoiling. Unless there is some way for a man to dispose of his surplus crops before they spoil, he will surely grow no more than his own family can consume; if he grows more, the surplus will only rot or be taken from him by others. Thus there will be no surplus, which is the necessary basis for the improvement of man's condition, and no "increase of mankind," which is the main intention of nature.

In brief, what was needed was some invention that would make it reasonable for a man to produce more than was necessary for his own family's immediate wants, more than they could consume before it spoiled. That invention was money, which, according to Locke, came into existence through a natural sort of progression. Men first bartered perishable foods for more durable foods, like nuts; later they traded goods for "a piece of metal, pleased with its color" (§46). Finally they arrived at an agreement that scarce but durable things, like gold and silver, would be taken in exchange for the perishable goods.

> And thus came in the use of money, some lasting thing that men might keep without spoiling, and that by mutual consent men would take in exchange for the truly useful but perishable supports of life [§47].

By this invention of money, men solved the basic economic problems of their original condition—with what far-reaching political consequences we shall presently see.

It is important to understand that Locke did indeed mean that money came into use before civil society. The use of money came in "by mutual consent" (§47) that men would exchange it for perishable goods. This "tacit and voluntary consent" does not presuppose the existence of civil society; it was made "out of the bounds of society and without compact, only by putting a value on gold and silver, and tacitly agreeing in the use of money . . ." (§50). This tacit agreement could not in itself establish civil society,

> for it is not every compact that puts an end to the state of nature between men, but only this one of agreeing together mutually to enter into one community and make one body politic; other promises and compacts men may make one with another and yet still be in the state of nature [§14].

Money was introduced in the natural common, but its use hastened the end of the natural common. Money so altered the conditions that it was no longer possible for men to live together without greater protection for their possessions. Money enabled men to enlarge their possessions; money made it profitable for a man to "possess more land than he himself can use the product of" (§50). Without money a man can have no incentive to enlarge his holdings and produce a surplus, however favorable all other circumstances may be:

> Where there is not something both lasting and scarce, and so valuable to be hoarded up, there men will not be apt to enlarge their possessions of land, were it never so rich, never so free for them to take [§48].

But "find out something that hath the use and value of money amongst his neighbors, you shall see the same man will begin presently to enlarge his possessions" (§49).

Introduction of the use of money completes the reversal of all of the original economic conditions. Unowned land becomes scarce because enclosed holdings are enlarged. The increased production can support an increased population, that is, a more plentiful labor supply. The early condition, in which possession was limited to "a very moderate proportion" (§36), gives way to larger possessions. The prevailing equality of penury is replaced by an economic inequality: "as different degrees of industry were apt to give men possessions in different proportions, so this invention of money gave them the opportunity to continue and enlarge them" (§48). Locke, we see, has done more than he promised; he has not only shown the origin of private property, he has justified the inequality of possessions:

> . . . it is plain that men have agreed to a disproportionate and unequal possession of the earth, they having, by a tacit and voluntary consent, found out a way how a man may fairly possess more land than he himself can use the product of, by receiving in exchange for the overplus, gold and silver, which may be hoarded up without injury to anyone, these metals not spoiling or decaying in the hands of the possessor. This partage of things in an inequality of private

possessions, men have made practicable . . . only by putting a value on gold and silver, and tacitly agreeing in the use of money [§50].

If we now consider the objection that might be most appropriately raised at this point—that an inequality of possessions is *not* fair—we are led directly to the central theme of Locke's whole political teaching: *increase*. The conditions of the first stages of the natural common were hostile to any prospects for increase in the supplies of goods men need for their comfort, convenience, and preservation. The question then was how to share the very little that could be wrested from the tight fist of nature. This meant that whoever took a little more than his neighbors "took more than his share and robbed others" (§46). When some men, by invention and industry, created the new conditions for the production of plenty, there came to be very much more to share; and although the new conditions required an inequality of possessions proportionate to the "different degrees of industry" among men, no one was cheated. Those who had a smaller share of the greatly increased whole were better off than those who had earlier shared, on an equal basis, in the pitiful little of the original condition. The poorest of men in a society having agriculture and money is richer than the most fortunate in the primitive, pre-agricultural natural common. Consider the "needy and wretched" Indians in America, who do not cultivate the soil: "a *king* of a large and fruitful territory there feeds, lodges, and is clad worse than a *day-laborer* in England" (§41, italics added).

It is difficult to exaggerate the importance Locke ascribed to the combination of agriculture and money. As he described the problem in an early essay, nature is utterly powerless to provide the conditions in which nature's own main intention—the increase of mankind—might be fulfilled:

> The inheritance of the whole of mankind is always one and the same, and it does not grow in proportion to the number of people born. Nature has provided a definite profusion of goods for the use and convenience of men, and the things brought forth have been bestowed in a definite manner and quantity deliberately; they have not been fortuitously produced nor are they increasing in proportion with men's need or avarice. . . . Whenever either the desire or the need of possession increases among men, there is no extension, then and there, of the world's limits. Victuals, clothes, adornments, riches, and all other good things of this life have been given in common; and when any man snatches for himself as much as he can, he takes away from another man's heap the

amount he adds to his own, and it is impossible for anyone
to grow rich except at the expense of someone else.[4]

This passage may be said to state the problem that Locke solved in the
Two Treatises. The world remains constant; it is not within nature's
power to extend its limits by even one square yard. But without such
extension, how can there ever be sufficient support for the increase of
mankind? How can there be any improvement in the condition of
men generally if "no gain falls to you which does not involve some-
body else's loss"?[5] The answer Locke provides is shocking in its
audacity. What is completely beyond the power of nature is well
within the power of *any* farmer:

> . . . he who appropriates land to himself by his labor does
> not lessen but increase the common stock of mankind. For
> the provisions serving to the support of human life produced
> by one acre of enclosed and cultivated land are (to speak
> much within compass) ten times more than those which are
> yielded by an acre of land of an equal richness lying waste in
> common. And therefore he that encloses land, and has a
> greater plenty of the conveniences of life from ten acres than
> he could have from a hundred left to nature, *may truly be said
> to give ninety acres to mankind* [§37, italics added].

Men, by their labor, invention, and arts, make *increase* possible
and thereby solve the economic problems that beset them in the
original natural condition. But at the same time they also make the
continuance of that state impossible. The original common, however
dangerous and inconvenient, is tolerable when its conditions are a
plenty of raw provisions, few men, lots of room, and a general
equality of weakness. But the consequences of *increase* are to make
unowned provisions scarcer, men more numerous, and open space
harder to come by; in this new situation a new inequality of power is
generated among men, based on the new inequality of possessions.
Under these new conditions labor can no longer give title to property
or be the measure of value, and spoiling ceases to limit acquisition.
Now for the first time there is the possibility of possessions too
extensive to protect by the means available in a state of nature. The
sovereignty of nature dissolves, and men must institute a new form of
rule of their own making to take its place. Men are "quickly driven
into society" (§127) for the protection of their property.

The possessions of the "industrious and rational"—those men
upon whose powers of increase the well-being of all depends—must
be protected from the "fancy or covetousness of the quarrelsome and
contentious" (§34). The final step in the long process of the liberation

of man's powers of increase from the restraints of nature is government. "The increase of lands and the right employing of them is the great art of government," and the prince is called "godlike" who "by established laws of liberty [secures] protection and encouragement to the honest industry of mankind. . . ."[6]

Locke's discussion of property is an account of the development of the original natural economic condition through several stages to the point where men can no longer live together without the authority and power of a common judge to protect the enlarged possessions made possible, to the benefit of all, after the introduction of money. Locke's theory of property explains the necessity for the transition from the state of nature to civil society.

11
Locke's State of Nature in Political Society

Readers of the *Two Treatises of Government* have long wondered about the meaning of Locke's discussion of the state of nature. Did Locke think that the state of nature really existed, or did he present it as an invented or imagined state? The question has been put in this form: Is Locke's state of nature moral fiction, historical fact, a combination of both, or something else?[1] I shall argue that, for Locke:

- The state of nature is a fact, not fiction.
- The state of nature is a fact of the present and the future as well as of the past (and is therefore not "historical" in the sense of something once but no longer existing).
- The state of nature is no more or less moral than anything else in the *Two Treatises of Government* (a work distinguished from most of Locke's other writings by the complete absence of the words "moral," "morals," and "morality").
- The state of nature is not only a persistent fact but a necessary and pervasive component of political life.

The Absence of Authority

Almost at the beginning of the *Second Treatise*, Locke presents his definition of political power and immediately thereafter says that "to understand political power right . . . we must consider what state all men are naturally in."[2] The state we are all naturally in, the state of nature, is essentially an unpolitical state. Locke thus begins his political argument with a profoundly paradoxical assertion: to understand what he means by political we must begin with consideration of the unpolitical. Why? What, in Locke's thought, is the connection of the unpolitical and the political? the state of nature and political power?

Locke gives us statements descriptive of the state of nature, for example, that in it all men are perfectly equal and perfectly free and that in it every man has the right to judge and punish violations of the law of nature, but these descriptive statements do not define the state of nature.[3] The essential defining characteristic of the state of nature is a defect—the lack of an authority, commonly accepted, to settle controversies that may arise. "Want of a common judge with authority puts all men in a state of nature."[4] The state of nature is governed by the law of nature,[5] but Locke makes it clear from the beginning of his argument and increasingly emphatic as it progresses that because judging and punishing are in the hands of every man, the state of nature works very badly: the law is insufficiently known and accepted as binding, the "judges" are biased, and enforcement of judgments is weak and uncertain.[6] Controversies in the state of nature, once begun, tend to continue to a harsh ending, because there is no authority to subject both parties "to the fair determination of the law."[7] "Some men have confounded" the state of nature and the state of war,[8] but Locke is careful to keep them separate in thought and definition. Although he gives many instances of aggressive violence in the state of nature, throughout the book Locke never says that the state of nature is a state of war, as Hobbes did.[9]

The state of nature and the state of war are not the same, but neither are they opposites. The opposite of the state of nature is civil society. Civil society is formed by the act of agreeing to supply what the state of nature lacks—a common judge with authority to settle controversies and punish violators of the law of that society. The state of nature and civil society are thus perfect opposites, each defined by the absence or the presence of a judge with authority.

The state of war is defined as the state men are in when one uses force without authority against the person of another; this is more likely to happen where there is no authoritative judge, but it can and does happen also within civil society. "Force without right upon a man's person makes a state of war, both where there is and is not a common judge."[10]

The opposite of the state of war would be a state of peace (mentioned once by Locke but not discussed),[11] characterized by the use of force only with right or—not precisely the same thing—the nonuse of force without right. In sum, the state of nature and the state of war are not the same, and they are not opposites; they are different states defined in dissimilar terms and therefore not truly comparable.

If this much is clear, we are ready to dispel several common confusions. The state of nature need not be prehistoric or a condition peculiar to primitive men or even prepolitical. Locke says that "all princes and rulers of independent governments" are in a state of nature.[12] By this example Locke shows that when he speaks of the state of nature we need not read into it more than Locke's own strictly limited definition: "Want of a common judge with authority puts all men in a state of nature." The phrase "state of nature," if it must conjure up images, should put the reader in mind of Queen Elizabeth, for example, perhaps more than of a caveman. Heads of governments, persons preeminently political, are denizens of the state of nature.

Further, men in the state of nature need not be thought of as either belligerent or pacific; the state of nature is the natural state of "all men." The state of nature is not limited to any era, prehistoric or historic; "the world never was, nor ever will be, without numbers of men in that state."[13] (Later we shall see that the state of nature exists not only between political communities but also within political communities.) The state of nature, in some form, always exists.

The state of war, also, is not necessarily unpolitical; it can exist in civil society. One of Locke's first examples of the state of war is of a thief and his victim, both members of the same political society:

> . . . force, or a declared design of force upon the person of another, where there is no common superior on earth to appeal to for relief [that is, in the state of nature], is the state of war: and 'tis the want of such an appeal gives a man the right of war even against an aggressor, though he be in society and a fellow subject [that is, in civil society].[14]

Thus, paradoxically, Locke asserts that men can be in a political and unpolitical state simultaneously; fellow subjects in political society can also be, *at the same time,* in a state of nature; and in that state of nature within civil society they can also be, *at the same time,* in a state of war with each other. How this works is made clearer by Locke's example:

> . . . a thief, whom I cannot harm but by appeal to the law, for having stolen all that I am worth, I may kill, when he sets on me to rob me but of my horse or coat: because the law, which was made for my preservation, where it cannot interpose to secure my life from present force . . . permits me my own defence, and the right of war, a liberty to kill the aggressor, because the aggressor allows not time to appeal to our common judge. . . .[15]

When one citizen, attacked by others, is unprotected by civil authority because the police cannot arrive in time, it is as if civil authority temporarily does not exist and, to a limited extent and temporarily, the citizens are in the state of nature although they are also, to a greater extent and permanently, in civil society. If in that situation of the state of nature within civil society unauthorized force is used against the person of some citizen or citizens, both the aggressors and the victims are in the state of war.

Because even in a strictly policed society the police cannot always be present, it is a common experience to be in the state of nature—as when walking down a dark and empty street at night one sees a strange figure approach and finds himself hoping that a police car will come by. As such occasions are common in the experience of us all, it is safe to say that everyone has been in the state of nature at one time or another, to some extent, even though he lives in civil society and always has.

Thus we see that the state of nature exists in two ways consistent with the existence of civil society: in the relations of independent political communities and, within a political community, in the relations of criminals and their victims. But the most significant form of the state of nature within civil society extends much further than these, to all those relations among men that should not be—and in a decent modern political society are not—regulated by the official authorities. Examples of such relations are the making and breaking of friendships, the making and breaking of promises that fall short of contracts, and the activities of business competition not involving violations of the law. These and similar activities and relations among men and women are thought to be beyond the proper reach of the authorities and are therefore a form of the state of nature within civil society, according to Locke's definition: "want of a common judge with authority puts all men in a state of nature."

Self-Preservation and the Preservation of All

This discussion of the state of nature has thus far ignored one explicit element of Locke's definition that should no longer be ignored. Locke says that "men living together *according to reason*, without a common superior on earth, with authority to judge between them, is properly the state of nature,"[16] and so we must ask what, in the state of nature, is "according to reason." In the state of nature two obligations dominate: everyone is "bound to preserve himself" and also "to preserve the rest of mankind." We cannot understand fully what Locke means by reason in the state of nature until we see how these two obligations are related. Locke says:

> Every one as he is bound to preserve himself, and not to quit his station willfully; so by the like reason when his own preservation comes not in competition, ought he, as much as he can, to preserve the rest of mankind, and may not unless

it be to do justice on an offender, take away, or impair the
life, or what tends to the preservation of the life, the liberty,
health, limb or goods of another.[17]

There are two seemingly equal obligations—to preserve yourself and
to preserve others. The first natural question (especially when the
author himself speaks of one's own preservation being "in competition") we must ask is, If they conflict, which comes first? Locke does
not raise that question explicitly, but he does provide the answer,
somewhat scattered throughout the *Two Treatises*.[18]

We must begin by noting that Locke places some qualifications on
the obligation to preserve the rest of mankind. Everyone ought to
preserve "the rest of mankind" "as much as he can"; in the state of
nature, how much *can* he? Everyone ought to seek to preserve "the
rest of mankind" "when his own preservation comes not in competition"; in the state of nature, will his own preservation come in competition often, and what must he do when it does? These qualifications
generate questions that make the equality of the two obligations
doubtful, at least, and suggest the possibility that Locke meant that
when the two obligations are in conflict, the duty of self-preservation
comes first. I shall argue, however, that that is not a sufficiently
accurate way of stating what Locke meant.

Self-preservation is a fundamental theme of the *Two Treatises*.
God's way of speaking to man and assuring him that everything he
does to preserve himself is right was to "plant" in man "a strong
desire of self-preservation."

> For the desire, strong desire of preserving his life and being
> having been planted in him, as a principle of action by God
> himself, reason, which was the voice of God in him, could
> not but teach him and assure him, that pursuing that natural
> inclination he had to preserve his being, he followed the will
> of his Maker, and therefore had a right . . . to make use of
> those things, that were necessary or useful to his being.[19]

The desire for self-preservation, Locke says, is "the first and strongest
desire,"[20] a "principle of action" implanted in us. Reason teaches us
that following the inclination to self-preservation is right; reason
"could not but teach" us and "assure" us of that. The most powerful
desire—for self-preservation—is the foundation of our right to life:
this is what reason teaches us. Locke's assertion that men live together
in the state of nature "according to reason" means that every man
seeks to protect his right to those things that tend to preserve his life.

If reason cannot teach us otherwise than that we have a right to
whatever we need for preservation, why do we need further instruc-

tion? One response might be that restraint and moderation and consideration for the preservation of others, being peaceable and nonprovocative ways of behaving toward others, are conducive to one's own preservation; if so, then men would very much need such instruction. We can say, then, that there are two aspects to self-preservation: first, caring for one's self and, second, respecting the right to life of others. The first is fully guided by the strongest human desire and by reason; the second requires instruction.

The state of nature is governed by the law of nature, and "reason, which is that law, teaches all mankind who will but consult it, that . . . no one ought to harm another. . . ." This is the part of the law of nature for which consulting, instruction, is needed. Are the conditions propitious for such consulting in the state of nature? Locke makes us doubt it: "For though the law of nature be plain and intelligible to all rational creatures; yet men being biassed by their interest, as well as ignorant for want of study of it, are not apt to allow of it as a law binding to them. . . ."[21] It seems that in the aspect of the law of nature in which men most need instruction—regard for the preservation of the rest of mankind—the state of nature provides poor professors.

To the extent that instructed reason teaches men to respect others, it will be little heeded in the state of nature. The difficulty is in that "first and strongest desire." Especially in the state of nature, that powerful natural inclination will be consistently operative. It should not surprise us that Locke nowhere tells us of a strong desire or natural inclination or principle of action within men to preserve the rest of mankind. He says we have that obligation, but what will lead us or force us to fulfill it? Locke's answer, I believe, is that only human law, in political society, will lead to the enforcement of that part of our natural obligations. "The obligations of the law of nature, cease not in society, but only in many cases are drawn closer, and have by human laws known penalties annexed to them, to inforce their observation."[22] Paradoxically, the law of nature—reason—becomes more fully operative in civil society than it can be in the state of nature.

To understand what Locke means by the phrase "according to reason," I asked the question: In case of conflict, which obligation comes first, the duty to preserve ourselves or the duty to preserve the rest of mankind? If I understand Locke correctly, his response would be that my question is not well put.

The end of the law of nature is the preservation of all mankind.[23] In the state of nature the enforcement of the law is in the hands of every man individually, for someone must have the authority to enforce the law and punish violators, or else it will not be effective;

and if one has such power in a state of perfect equality, all must have it.[24] The law of nature, which wills the preservation of all mankind, is soon transformed by Locke into preservation of "the innocent" and restraint of "offenders"[25]—quite sensibly, of course, for if there were not both kinds of men there would be no problem of preservation or at least no need to protect men from the hostility of other men, although there would still be the problems occasioned by the harshness of nature, such as famine, epidemic, flood, drought, or earthquake. The task then becomes not to preserve all, which is not always possible, but to avoid the victory of the "offenders" at the expense of the preservation of "the innocent";[26] the problem then becomes one of determining the extent to which "one man may lawfully do harm to another."[27]

A man who attacks another without right "becomes dangerous to mankind"; his assault is "a trespass against the whole species." The one who is attacked may kill the attacker "where it is necessary," and in doing so he acts "by the right he hath to preserve mankind in general."[28] In the state of nature "every man . . . has a power to kill a murderer," because a murderer has "declared war against all mankind."[29] The "right to destroy that which threatens me with destruction" is justified in the name of the obligation to preserve all: "For by the fundamental law of nature, man being to be preserved, as much as possible, when all cannot be preserv'd, the safety of the innocent is to be preferred. . . ."[30]

The turn of the argument is now apparent. The question of the priority of self-preservation *versus* the preservation of all seems to dissolve as Locke argues it. There need be no answer to the question in that form, because the two obligations appear to merge and become almost one. In the state of nature and in the state of nature in civil society, when one defends himself against attack, he defends all of mankind as well as himself. If he kills the aggressor, he has saved himself and protected mankind: "One may destroy a man who makes war upon him . . . for the same reason that he may kill a wolf or a lyon."[31]

If I am not mistaken, in *every* passage in which Locke speaks of the duty to preserve all mankind, he invariably links the performance of that obligation to the *killing* of another man who might endanger one's life.[32] Even when he is speaking of men not in the state of nature, we see the same pattern:

> [Political power is] a power to make laws, and annex such penalties to them, as may tend to the preservation of the whole [society], but cutting off those parts, and those only, which are so corrupt, that they threaten the sound and

healthy, without which no severity is lawful.[33]

Locke's assumption everywhere is that there will inevitably be offenders against the law seeking the preservation of all and that therefore the preservation of all is unattainable; he seeks what might be attainable, the preservation of some, "the innocent," by the killing of the offenders ("where it is necessary").[34] But because a chief characteristic of the state of nature is the self-love that makes men partial to themselves, the inclination is strong for every man to judge himself to be one of "the innocent" and others to be the offenders: "where men may be judges in their own case, . . . he who was so unjust as to do his brother an injury, will scarce be so just as to condemn himself for it."[35] I conclude that in the state of nature everything a man does to preserve himself is likely to be justified by him, the sole judge and executioner, as action to punish an aggressor or offender against the law of nature. Preserving one's self and preserving all mankind thus become practically indistinguishable.

If there were a more readily discernible conflict between the two great natural obligations, surely self-preservation, the one buttressed by "the first and strongest desire," would prevail. Mankind is fortunate that the preservation of all of mankind can be linked by reason to the powerful natural inclination to self-preservation.

The State of Nature and the State of War

The strong desire for self-preservation, according to Locke, is the foundation of the natural right to things conducive to preservation; given that right, reason teaches everyone in the state of nature that he has a right to kill another man who threatens him, as much as he has the right to kill an attacking wild animal. Because this has so harsh a sound, it bears repeating that the state of nature according to Locke is different from Hobbes's state of nature. Hobbes rarely used the phrase "the state of nature"; it never occurs in *Leviathan*, if I am not mistaken (although other very similar phrases do occur, such as "the condition of mere nature"). When he speaks of life being "solitary, poor, nasty, brutish, and short," Hobbes is speaking expressly of the "time of war."[36] But Hobbes does not differentiate the states or conditions of nature and war. For example, in *De Cive*, Hobbes says that "the state of men without civil society (which state we may properly call the state of nature) is nothing else but a mere war of all against all. . . ."[37] In another place in the same work, he says, "we mean such a war as is of all men against all men, such as is the mere state of nature."[38] The point of this textual observation is not so much to say something

117

about Hobbes as to emphasize the significance of the distinction of the two states so carefully defined and so strictly adhered to by Locke. Locke made a use of the state of nature that Hobbes did not, by separating it, by definition, from the state of war.

When Locke speaks of men in the state of nature the reader can substitute the definition "Men living together according to reason, without a common superior" without having to add any other condition or characteristic. It can be a state of any sort or sorts of men, as long as they lack an effective and commonly accepted authority. Or they can be men in civil society whose relations are none of the business of the authorities or beyond the reach of the authorities. As long as there is no authority to intervene in case of controversy, they are—at least in part or temporarily or both—in the state of nature.

The State of Nature and Political Power

The state of nature and the state of war are mentioned more frequently toward the end of the *Second Treatise*, where political society is discussed, than in many early chapters of the book that discuss the life of man outside political society. This observation brings us back to the earlier question: What is the political relevance of the unpolitical?

In the state of nature a man has two great natural powers: first, not surprisingly, the power to preserve his own life, liberty, and possessions; second, the power to "punish the breaches of that law [of nature] in others, as he is perswaded the offence deserves, even with death. . . ."[39] These two powers are the "original" of political power; they are the natural powers given up to form civil society. But one of these powers is not and cannot be wholly given up; what is retained by every man, what is held back even in civil society, gives a special character to Locke's teaching about the nature of the political.

The power each man has in the state of nature "to punish the crimes committed against that law [of nature]," Locke says, "he wholly gives up."[40] There cannot be civil society where citizens continue to insist on their natural right to punish those who violate the law. The earlier example of the thief made this clear; even if he steals "all that I am worth," "I cannot harm [him] but by appeal to the law."

It is otherwise with the first natural power, "*viz.* of doing whatsoever he thought fit for the preservation of himself, and the rest of mankind. . . ."[41] Locke does not say that this power is *wholly* given up in order to form political society. Whenever he speaks of this first natural power, he qualifies the giving up. It is clear that the power of self-preservation cannot be given up completely; something of it persists within civil society. He says that every man gives up this power "so far forth as the preservation of himself, and the rest of that society shall require."[42] This must be contrasted with the words that follow immediately: "Secondly, the power of punishing he wholly gives up. . . ."[43]

The first reservation concerns the ability of the authorities to act and act in time. The natural power is "resign'd up into the hands of the community in all cases that exclude him not from appealing for protection to the law."[44] It cannot be considered wholly given up because there will be cases where appeal for effective protection is not possible. Again: "with the judgment of offences which he has given up to the legislative in all cases, where he can appeal to the magistrate, he has given a right to the commonwealth to imploy his force. . . ."[45] Because there will be cases where he cannot appeal to the magistrate, the right is not wholly given up. Once again:

> Now this power, which every man has in that state of nature, and which he parts with to the society, in all cases, where the society can secure him, is, to use such means for the preserving of his own property, as he thinks good, and nature allows him. . . .[46]

Since society will not be able to secure him in every case, it is clear that something is held back by every man in the transition from the state of nature to civil society.

This something held back is the retained natural power of every citizen to do whatever seems necessary to preserve himself in all those cases where he can rely on no one but himself; there must be many such cases, as we have seen, in the common experience of everyone. But Locke's use of it goes much further than the right of self-defense against an armed robber. The greatest threat to self-preservation in civil society is the man who abuses political power and attempts to extend it beyond political limits. When a ruler uses power in a way that makes the people feel unsafe, when their lives, liberties, and estates are in danger of confiscation or are subject to other illegal force and there is, in the nature of the situation, no appeal to an impartial judge with authority to settle the controversy between the ruler and subjects, that something held back comes into decisive action. The law they will act under, the law of self-preservation, is "a law antecedent and paramount to all positive laws of men." They have "reserv'd that ultimate determination to themselves, which belongs to all mankind, where there lies no appeal on earth."

> And this judgment they cannot part with, it being out of a man's power so to submit himself to another, as to give him a liberty to destroy him; God and Nature never allowing a man

119

so to abandon himself, as to neglect his own preservation; and since he cannot take away his own life, neither can he give another power to take it.[47]

The significance of the state of nature—or the remnant of it that survives in that portion of natural power that every man holds back—in civil society is the limitation it places on the exercise of political power. The tyrant uses power that was not given up to him and to the community. The people sense the danger to themselves and their property. He uses their force for purposes they never intended, for his good, not theirs. The tyrant places himself outside their political society, because he puts himself above the law, and men are not in the same political society unless they are subject to the same laws and to the same common judge. The tyrant is in the state of nature in relation to the subjects, and if he uses force against them, it will be without right; thus he puts himself in a state of war with them, in which state they have the right to defend themselves and to do whatever they think aids their own preservation.[48]

Something of the state of nature persists within every man, in that part of his right to protect himself that he cannot give up without becoming something less than a human being; Locke describes this sort of man, lifeless though alive, in his chapter "Of Slavery."[49] Slaves are not proprietors of their own lives; they have nothing to hold back. Men who are not slaves hold back something from political society that they do not and cannot give up, no matter how civilized and politicized they are.

Thus the state of nature persists in civil society in two ways. The first survival of it is seen in the fact that civil authority cannot reach everywhere. If a political regime did seek to be completely totalitarian, that is, to regulate the totality of human affairs, not only patrolling every street but penetrating behind every closed door (or, more extreme, removing every lock or even every door that might be closed to surveillance), even so the state of nature would not be completely eradicated; in fact, according to Locke's argument, it would be reintroduced in a stronger and worse form than the ordinary state of nature. The totalitarian attempt to eradicate the state of nature within political society is not political at all; it uses power that cannot be called political because it is a use of power that men cannot consent to; it puts the authorities in a state of nature with the subject; it brings back the state of nature and the state of war, this time with no admixture of political society. Locke says of absolute monarchy that it is "inconsistent with civil society, and so can be no form of civil government at all."[50] The attempt of a dictator to stamp out the vestiges of natural right or power within civil society has the opposite of the intended effect: it brings back the full state of nature; it eliminates civil society; it is the worst form of the state of nature, because it is combined with the state of war.[51]

The second way in which the state of nature must persist in civil society lies in that simple fact of human nature, according to Locke, that men cannot wholly give up their desire or natural inclination to look out for themselves, an inclination that is strengthened by danger.[52] Something of the state of nature persists within every citizen; driving it out of him does not make him more of a citizen but the opposite; adhering strictly to Locke's definitions and terms, we must see that a successful purging of the remnant of the state of nature from a citizen would make him not more of a citizen but a slave.

The Necessity of Restraint and Moderation

A proper understanding of what Locke means by the state of nature, limiting it to the state as defined by Locke and not adding unnecessary accretions of meaning, reveals why the phrase appears so often when Locke speaks of the "executive prerogative," "tyranny," the limits of political power, "the right to resist" the tyrant, and the "dissolution of government." Perhaps the most important aspect for us is the way in which Locke used the term and the thought to set out the limits of political power. The teaching must be understood as addressed to both the rulers and the ruled. To both the admonition is to beware of bringing back the full state of nature[53] in a worse form than the ordinary state of nature. The teaching to both is one of restraint and moderation.

The ruler who understands that something of the state of nature persists within every subject or citizen, and that something of the state of nature persists also in the relations among *all* men and women in a political society, will be restrained in the exercise of his authority. He will be tolerant of that uncivilized remnant of natural liberty within political society and within every citizen. He will be aware that the effort to make political society completely civil cannot succeed; it can only have the result of putting the ruler outside the society of his subjects or of making them slaves. He will understand, that is, that the political, by definition and deduction, cannot be all-pervasive, and so he will not seek to accomplish the impossible.

The people, also, if they understand the political relevance of the state of nature, will be restrained in their political action. Their awareness of the remnant of the state of nature within civil society and within each of them will make them alert to the danger of excessive use of power by the authorities. If they wish to forestall a

121

return to the full state of nature, they will be moderate in their claims to that portion of natural power still in their own possession. Civil society is formed, after all, by wholly giving up the power to punish crimes; that is, persons taught by Locke would always be opposed to the notion of taking the law into their own hands as long as the government was functioning with right and authority. Citizens are in danger of bringing back the full state of nature with all its unendurable hardships by claiming the right to use powers they had in the state of nature and gave up to form civil society. The fact that something is reserved is consistent with the teaching that practically all the natural powers of every man and woman have been given up to the community.

The stability and decency of political society depend on restraint and moderation on the part of both political leaders and citizenry. Where will political wisdom and moderation come from? The task of political leaders in a society guided by Lockean teachings is to support laws and institutions and doctrines that preserve and protect the remnant of the state of nature within political society and within every citizen, because the effort to stamp out every trace of it has the result of returning all to the full state of nature. It is their task, also, to discourage the extension of the state of nature beyond civil limits, as if we had given up nothing to escape the full state of nature and enjoy the peace, plenty, and freedom of political society.

The greatest danger to civil society can be summed up as the danger of falling back into a full state of nature, in a worse form than the ordinary one. On one side of civil society lies tyranny, a state of nature disguised as political society; on the other side lies anarchy or civil war, another form of the full state of nature, the result of excessive use of natural powers on the part of the people. Only moderation and restraint and understanding can save political society from calamity on one side or the other. Civil society is a mean between two extremes—and both extremes are the state of nature.

PART FOUR

International Diplomacy—
Who Owns the Unowned?

12
Locke and the Law of the Sea

Powerful individuals and nations rarely have much need of philosophy; it is not usual for ignorance of philosophy to cost them much, if anything. But in 1981 there was such a rare moment in history, a moment when access to resources estimated to be worth billions of dollars depended on the right interpretation of an old philosophic formulation—that the oceans are "the common heritage of mankind." The nations of the world, 160 of them, had assented to this principle as the foundation of the United Nations Conference on the Law of the Sea, which had been going on at least since 1973. The draft of a treaty near completion had been described as the single most extensive and complicated international agreement ever devised: among other things it would establish an elaborate, autonomous governmental structure, the International Seabed Authority—complete with an assembly, a council, several commissions, a secretariat, a "disputes chamber," and its own mining operation—with sweeping jurisdiction over "the Area" (the deep seas). This immense international organization would rest on two succinct sentences in the treaty: "the Area and its resources are the common heritage of mankind," and "All rights in the resources of the Area are vested in mankind as a whole, on whose behalf the Authority shall act."

In all the deliberations of scores of nations, in thousands of hours of negotiation, hammering out compromise after compromise involving billions of dollars of future business, little if any attention was given to the question of what it means to say that the oceans are "the common heritage of mankind."

This is not at all a new question in philosophy. It was raised and well answered three hundred years ago; so one would assume that at least some of those who negotiated on behalf of the commercial nations and the corporations involved would be familiar with it. Yet the spokesmen of the West went into the law of the sea negotiations with an idea about "the common heritage of mankind" contrary to the truth and contrary to their obvious self-interest. This misinterpretation had been advanced, year after year, by three successive U.S. presidents, by a parade of diplomatic spokesmen, and by numerous supposedly sensible business leaders, not only of the United States but of just about all the modern industrial nations. They marched right to the brink and were pulled back only at the last moment, just as the tenth session of the Law of the Sea Conference was to begin at the United Nations in New York.

On March 2, 1981, the State Department announced that Secretary of State Alexander M. Haig had "instructed our representative to the UN Law of the Sea Conference to seek to insure that the negotiations do not end at the present session of the conference, pending policy review by the United States government." On April 14, a U.S. delegate said that the United States would prefer to delay final resolution on the international sea law treaty at least until the fall and probably until 1982.

When the Reagan administration called this halt and insisted on a review, we were inches from agreeing to some or all of the following: that mining companies could invest billions of dollars to scoop up the nodules of manganese, copper, nickel, and cobalt that lie at the bottom of the sea only as licensed by the new International Seabed Authority; that they would have to pay the authority for the privilege; that they would have to put the Authority's own operating company (called the Enterprise) into business with capital and technology; that the United States and other developed nations would have a minimal voice in the Authority; and that all disputes, regulations, and production levels (and hence prices and profits) would be set by one or another organ of the Authority.

After so many years of pledging "to regard these resources as the common heritage of mankind" (President Richard Nixon, 1970) and of interpreting "the common heritage" to mean "that the resources don't belong to any nation, but to the world community as a whole" (Ambassador Elliot Richardson, 1981), it would not do for the United States and its friends simply to say that they want a better deal for their efforts to scoop up the minerals from the depths. The only honorable route for the Reagan administration was to explain what the error has been—an error that all the nations have shared in—and to begin the necessary task of negotiating new laws of the sea from a sounder interpretation of "the common heritage of mankind."

The Universal Common

Hugo Grotius is generally acknowledged to have formulated first, in 1609, the argument that the oceans beyond territorial limits belong to mankind in common, and the phrase that came into use was "the universal common." The meaning was that no nation could claim control of the seas as they did then and do now over territorial waters and that therefore all have the right to traverse open seas for commerce and for fishing without being hindered or having to obtain anyone's permission.

Thoughtful writers saw that there is something not quite rigorous about the notion of a universal common, about something *belonging* to all mankind. Toward the end of the seventeenth century John Locke, in his *Two Treatises of Government*, pointed out that when we say something belongs to everyone, we really mean it does not belong to anyone. The use of the word "common" is what led to the confusion, and Locke sought to clarify matters by making an important distinction. Villages in England—and in many other countries, too—had what were called commons. In such a common no villager could claim a right to enclose or appropriate any part without the consent of his fellow villagers. But although "the universal common" was meant to be an analogy to the familiar village common, a village common differs from a universal common—a common of all mankind—in two decisive ways.

First, the village common is created by the law of the land—by positive, legislated, promulgated, enforceable law—and a universal common is not because international law is not really law but only agreed upon practice and custom.

Second, although the village common is common to the inhabitants of that village, it is not common to others; the village common is property, the joint property of the village, to the exclusion of all others. The notion of owning requires exclusion. Something is yours only if others cannot use it or consume it without your consent.

Locke, the great teacher of the theory of property, put it this way: "what fish anyone catches in the ocean, that great and still remaining common of mankind . . . is made his property who takes that pains about it." If we substitute the word "nodule" for "fish," cannot Locke's assertion be made even now, that the ocean is still a common of mankind (that is, unowned) and that therefore what nodules anyone scoops up are the property of those who take the pains—billions of dollars in investment and risk—to get them to the surface?

The answer I think Locke would give is no, not quite. In an economic situation, says Locke, where there is a great expanse of land or water that is unowned, containing a great abundance of natural materials—apples or fish or nodules—property in these natural things is accomplished simply by the effort or labor expended in acquiring them. Even in a universal common, each human being owns himself and his own labor; therefore, if he "mixes his labor,"

127

which is exclusively his, with the natural materials, which are un-owned, the mixture becomes his property. But Locke goes on to explain that this is true only when there is such an abundance of natural materials that whatever is appropriated leaves enough and as good for others.

In short, the argument about fish in the unowned waters being free for the taking and the property of whoever catches them satisfies us as a just and practical working rule as long as there is a great abundance of fish but comes into question as soon as it appears that the supply of fish is limited.

The same is true, in Locke's own argument, of all other resources. For example, it would be foolish to complain, in a spacious park on a clear and sparkling day, that someone in the crowd is exercising too strenuously and breathing too deeply and thus taking more than his fair share of oxygen. The reason is, in Locke's terms, that enough and as good is left for others. But if the same complaint were made in a disabled submarine lying at the bottom of the sea with a limited supply of oxygen and the rescue time uncertain, our judgment would be very different. No one would say that anyone may jump about and inhale as much as he pleases of the "common" oxygen; the reason is simply that what is left may not be enough for the others.

With these considerations in mind, it is not hard to see why nations felt an urgency about setting new rules for the uses of the oceans. From 1950 to 1974 the world harvest of fish grew more than fourfold; in the same twenty-five-year period merchant ship tonnage also increased fourfold. Then everyone acknowledged that a wholly new era was introduced with the discovery of oil under the continental shelf off the coast of the United States and of the nodules lying on the floor of the oceans at very great depths.

These changes in the intensity of use of the oceans and the extraction of their nonfish resources make it difficult, perhaps impossible, for the oceans to continue to be regarded as a universal common, unowned and unregulated. Mining the nodules is different from fishing, as Ambassador Richardson pointed out, because "deep sea-bed nodules can't swim, and sea-bed miners aren't fishermen. Miners must have an exclusive legal right to a suitable ore body before they undertake the large, long-term investments necessary to recover and process the ore."

In these new circumstances the dispute is not whether new rules are needed. The real disputes are—or should be—what rules, made by whom, supervised by whom, and for whose benefit? Thinking straight about the meaning of "the common heritage of mankind" gives guidance on the crucial questions: Who comes to the conference table to formulate the new rules and with what standing?

No Ownership

Let us go back to the beginning. When the assertion is made that the deep seas are the common heritage of mankind, it does not mean that every human being is a part owner of the international waters; much less can it mean that every nation considered sovereign is somehow a part owner. What it means is that the international waters are un-owned. Thus when something must be done to make sensible rules for the use of these waters and the resources in them, nations come to the conference table in the status of nonowners. No ownership is the problem in this case; no one has authority to govern the deep seas; yet certain kinds of activities on them or in them would be beneficial, activities that are usually conducted under conditions of ownership or sovereignty. The task is to figure out some way to end the inconve-niences inherent in a universal common, a situation without gover-nance or property. Instead of proclaiming that "the Area and its resources are the common heritage of mankind," the negotiators should face the fact that their task is to terminate the common for the sake of law and property.

The conference was conducted on a completely opposite basis. Nations came to the conference table as if they were stockholders, each with an equal share of stock and the equal voting right that goes with it. They took this formulation, "the common heritage of man-kind," to mean joint ownership; added the twist that the shares belonged to sovereign nations, not individuals; and went further and decided that each nation's share was equal regardless of population, location, or involvement in the production or consumption of the minerals.

By thus assuming a meaning of the founding principle that is the exact opposite of its true meaning, they foreordained the result of the conference before it even began. They asserted that the unowned seas were indeed owned, by them, one share per sovereign nation, whether they had a seacoast or not, whether they had a population big enough to fill a football stadium or not. Most amazing of all, they beguiled great commercial powers into believing them. They found the Achilles' heel of the great commercial powers—dire ignorance of the philosophical foundations of private property. So the swindle was launched on the seas—and named, with exquisite Orwellian irony, the Enterprise.

What Can Be Done?

The remedy is easier now that President Ronald Reagan and Secretary Haig have taken the first and most difficult step of stopping the headlong rush to disaster. Let the review begin, and let the United States formulate a position based on an honorable adherence to principle and sound interpretation.

We can start by announcing that we accept the principle that the deep seas are "that great and still remaining common of mankind," as our teacher Locke taught three centuries ago. Next, let us point out that the meaning of this principle, clear beyond dispute, is that until some agreement changes the status of the deep seas, no nation owns them or can prohibit taking anything from them. The seas being unowned, in the absence of new agreements the nodules are free for the taking, just as loose fish are in international waters, and no nation or international body has any right to interfere. Let us further point out that if the world is in need of natural resources, including those metals now lying useless (because unappropriated) at the bottom of the sea, we deprive all mankind of their benefit as long as we delay the mining of them.

There is thus an urgent task to be worked out at the conference table. Let nations properly concerned with these matters come together, but let it be understood that no nation can come to the table in the guise of a shareholder or with any kind of claim to owning what lies in these seas or to a right to hinder appropriation of the nodules, *because* they are "the common heritage of mankind." No nation has a *right* to any particular share; no nation has a predetermined voice or vote in what is to be done; no one has *any* authority until there is an agreement about what is to be done.

In short, the main corrective that results from a clearer understanding of what "the common heritage of mankind" means is that the status of the negotiators is altered. The Law of the Sea Conference cannot be a meeting of equal shareholders, each with one vote. It must be a meeting of nations coming together to decide who should have what to say about the rules that would govern the use of territory that is now unowned and therefore unregulated but that needs to be regulated.

Once the United States states clearly that it does not start from the principle that the permission of others is needed to remove nodules from unowned seas, it should reopen all the understandings tentatively reached regarding these deep seabed resources when it was under the misapprehension that it was participating in a shareholder's meeting. It should take a stance appropriate to a free commercial society and ask why the nodules should not be mined by private entrepreneurs for profit.

Until now the majority of the spurious "stockholders" have argued that if some of the nodules are mined by private firms, that must be done in tandem with mining by the Enterprise "for the good of the world community." The underlying theme was first enunciated by Arvid Pardo, the Maltese delegate to the United Nations, in 1967. Ambassador Pardo was the first in the United Nations to use the phrase "the common heritage of mankind" to describe the deep seas, and he is the one who described the task as a race between "the good of one" (meaning the nation-state acting in its own selfish interest) and "the common good" (meaning the United Nations and other international organizations).

Why should we, the United States and other exemplars of the democratic capitalist system, agree to such a distinction? It should be made as clear to the rest of the world as it is (or should be) to us that what justifies encouragement to private enterprises is that all society benefits.

Further, we should insist on reviewing the protectionist regulations proposed by the Authority to restrict competition with the manganese and other metals now mined in some third world countries. The draft treaty proposes that supplies and prices be regulated by an international body to preserve a "just" price and an orderly market. This translates into international governmental control over world commerce, founded on the conviction that government officials can manage a more rational system of production and distribution than a free market can. The least of the harmful effects would be higher prices throughout the world for manganese, copper, nickel, and cobalt. More important, however, would be the inordinate control over important activities placed in the hands of officials who have been self-selected and who are accountable primarily to themselves and other international bodies and officials but not to nations and peoples.

One more very important point ought to be reviewed by the United States and its friends before they go forward toward any treaty regarding rules governing the use of the seas. The elaborate system now incorporated in the draft treaty would provide income to the Authority through its operating arm, the Enterprise. The private mining companies would be required to set the Enterprise up in business, provide it with capital, technology, and a share of the mining business.

The whole arrangement is so complicated that many experts acknowledge that they do not understand it themselves. It is clear, nonetheless, that this new and autonomous arm of the United Nations, dominated by third world nations, is designed to have an ensured income of quite considerable size to be used "for the benefit of the world community." The officials of international organizations, the international civil servants who serve as staff and experts for organizations such as this proposed International Seabed Authority, have been searching for years for some means of obtaining funding without having to rely on the contributions of member nations, especially the members who make big contributions and most especially the member who makes the biggest contribution by far—the United States. If they could be free of reliance on what the United States puts in and then free of the strings that naturally result, the UN and other international organizations would have the independence for which they yearn. The report of the Brandt commission contains a proposal for international taxation, assured revenue provided by mathematical formula, some way to reduce the influence of rich members who control the purse strings. An income-producing business operation, tax-exempt and untouched by competition, would be even better.

With other people's capital and technology, the international civil servants would be put into business, and with the gain they would become independent. Part of the rules they developed and to which we were close to agreeing is control over the mining activities of the companies that have the technology. This would be a minor boon to some poor countries but a major boon to those who staff the international organizations. They are officials quite decisively separated from their native countries (in fact, that is an explicit provision for officials of the Authority and the Enterprise). What we have here, starting in the deepest parts of the ocean but with sweeping authority over almost all activities on the seas, is a large, complicated, highly organized, unelected, powerful government, with prospects for abundant funding that cannot be controlled or reduced or cut off. Americans ought not to cooperate in the establishment of any such "Enterprise."

Conclusion

These, then, are the principles with which the United States might consider a return to the Law of the Sea Conference. No doubt such a stance on our part would mean many more years of negotiating before agreement could be reached. Ambassador Richardson, when addressing the American Mining Congress, acknowledged that being right does not always mean that others will go along: "Our view, as you know, is that deep sea-bed resources may be recovered lawfully by any state or its nationals as an exercise of a traditional high-seas freedom. We see nodules as analogous to the living resources of the high seas—the fish—that are found beyond the two-hundred-mile fishery zone. This is not merely a defensible position but one that rests on a solid foundation of established international law. There are, however, difficulties with it. One is that it is totally rejected by most governments, including those of all the developing countries."

We should not abandon a position that is philosophically sound and rests on a solid foundation of established international law just because others disagree. If it is right and in our interest, we must persevere though we may not succeed. If we do succeed, it is probable that it will take years even so to persuade so many others.

For that reason a short deadline should be placed on commencing the mining of the nodules while negotiations proceed. Demands will be made that the new system must benefit the world community and not the corporations or the rich countries, but in the meantime the nodules remain at the bottom of the sea benefiting no one. In the interest of the world community, which suffers from a shortage of these metals, no more delay should be tolerated. Let the nations settle on temporary arrangements to make mining possible in accord with the principles set out here, and let it commence without delay as the conference continues deliberations.

If that cannot be done, then let the companies begin, with guarantees of protection from the United States and other nations willing to join in, until such time as the conference can settle on rules acceptable to all.

When the nodules are recovered, processed, and marketed and when the profits are reinvested and distributed to stimulate further development, as profits always must be, perhaps the corporations will consider investing a small portion of the surplus in sending their executives back to school to learn a little of the philosophical theory of the origins of private property and why they should not be hesitant in their assertions that profit serves the common good. The most profitable return of all would be for the spokesmen of the free commercial societies to learn how to explain the connection of economic liberty and political liberty to those who have neither and long for both.

13

Common Sense versus "The Common Heritage"

When President Ronald Reagan's decision was announced in March 1981 that the United States would not continue negotiations and would instead begin what turned out to be a lengthy review of the Law of the Sea Treaty, proponents of the treaty in the United States and elsewhere in the world were incredulous. Two years later, after completion of the review, after announcement of the "six objectives" that the United States sought and other nations did not agree to, and, finally, after announcement that the United States would not sign the treaty or participate in any future preparations or activities, the proponents of the treaty were still incredulous. They did not believe, they could not accept the thought, that the United States would not be a signatory.[1]

To them the benefits to the United States, as to the world, seem so obvious that they can offer only three possible explanations for President Reagan's actions: that he is ignorant,[2] that he is a rigid ideologue,[3] or that he is both.[4]

The argument I shall put forth suggests the reverse: it is the critics of the Reagan policy, the *proponents* of the Law of the Sea Treaty, who have allowed unthinking commitment to ideology to blind them to dominant facts that lie at the heart of the controversy over whether to sign the treaty. Let us turn directly to the questions that matter: What, if anything, is wrong with the treaty? Is there reason not to sign it? If we do not sign, what should we do?

Law of the Sea and Law of the Seabed

To begin to see what is wrong with the treaty, we must make a distinction so obvious that almost everyone either ignores or overlooks it. The treaty deals with two significantly different kinds of subject matter: one has to do with *the sea*, the other with *the deep seabed*. It deals with the former tolerably well and by acceptably sensible means. The latter it botches incredibly, in ways that are

134

simultaneously excessive, irrelevant, and potentially oppressive. The parts having to do with the sea—fishing, navigation, shipping, pollution control, marine research, and the like—are familiar subjects of international maritime agreements and are properly called the law of the sea. But the provisions having to do with the deep seabed are unprecedented in international agreements; they are an international novelty and should go under a different name, for the sake of clarity and truth: the law of the deep seabed. These provisions pertain only to the seabed of those waters beyond territorial limits or economic zones of any nation, beyond the continental shelf, and to the nonliving resources lying on the deep seabed. The specific nonliving resource that has been the object of attention of the negotiators for more than a decade has been the manganese nodules, estimated to be worth billions of dollars, just lying there at great depths, presumably waiting to be scooped, pumped, or sucked up, then to be transported, refined, and sold for immense gains.

This distinction between the sea and the deep seabed is the essential starting point for understanding what the problem is and what is at stake. All the controversy over whether to sign the treaty centers on the law of the deep seabed, none at all on the law of the sea. If the treaty dealt only with the law of the sea, the United States would have signed long ago. If the treaty were now stripped of the deep seabed provisions and no other word in the treaty were touched, the United States would sign without delay. The United States is not especially pleased with some provisions in the sea portions—some having to do with fishing, others with marine research—but on balance the spokesmen of the United States, especially President Reagan, have expressed themselves repeatedly as not merely satisfied but pleased with that major part of the text of the treaty.

There is nothing surprising in this. Few other nations have as much of a stake in the law-abiding, peaceful use of the oceans as the United States. Use of the oceans has increased too rapidly in recent decades. As a result, new problems have been generated and old ones intensified. It was obvious that some wholly new rules needed to be formulated, some existing rules needed strengthening, and in certain very important situations longstanding customary rules needed codification. The United States made useful, major contributions throughout these negotiations and was not unhappy with the results. President Reagan affirmed this in his statement announcing that the United States would not sign the treaty. He explained that the provisions dealing with the law of the sea contained "positive and very significant accomplishments." Most of the provisions, he said, "are consistent with United States interests and, in our view, serve well the interests of all nations."[5] In short, the United States would be a willing signatory if the law of the sea were the full subject matter of the Law of the Sea Treaty. But it is not; the law of the deep seabed is a part of it, too.

To implement the provisions of the treaty dealing with the principal activities of the world's oceans—fishing rights, navigation and overflight, pollution control, marine research, and similar matters— not one new international agency had to be brought into existence. But everything is quite different when we turn to the other part, the troublesome part of the treaty, the part that deals not with the sea but with the deep seabed and the inanimate things that rest on it. This part of the treaty announces a new doctrine of international control, if not international ownership, of hitherto unowned territories and establishes new institutions that rival the United Nations itself in size, scope, complexity, powers, and numbers of employees. There would be an assembly, a council, a secretariat, a number of expert commissions, courts of various sorts called disputes chambers, and a mining company called the Enterprise that would—on paper, at least—be equal in size, funding, and activity to all the competing private sea-mining consortia of the world *combined.*

Ill-founded Hopes

The obvious justification for a new law of the sea is the greatly intensified use of the seas by the nations of the world, which generates new problems that must be addressed constructively and that, on balance, have been so dealt with in the treaty. But what is the justification for the new law of the deep seabed? The answer given by treaty proponents is that the manganese nodules present a new problem and a new opportunity for global development and international economic justice.

To understand the deep seabed provisions of the treaty, it is necessary to try to recapture the aspirations and expectations of the negotiators in the 1960s and 1970s. The assumption was that the manganese nodules were a source of tremendous riches and that, unless strict precautions were taken and enforced with energy and vigilance, only the most wealthy and technologically advanced nations would profit from them. This gave birth to the doctrine of "the common heritage of mankind," interpreted to mean that the unowned and unacquired nodules already belonged to mankind as a whole and that each sovereign nation owned a share of the common property. By carefully drawn rules to be made, administered, and adjudicated by novel international agencies, the poorer nations would get a fair share of the immense profits, would acquire advanced technology, and would assume a new role in actually managing vast enterprises that would dwarf the most optimistic possibilities in their own smaller and poorer national economies. It sounds wonderful, but two things are wrong: the theory and the facts.

Three hundred years ago the argument was made that a universal commons (based on a false analogy to the familiar village commons) is impossible. A village commoner can help himself to much of what is common without seeking the consent of his fellow commoners, but the commons itself is property, joint property that excludes others who may not take what they please without permission. There can be no property, no ownership, without excluding others. Where others can take what they want without another's consent, there is no property. In short, to speak of the deep seabed as a universal or global commons either is nonsense, literally, or means that *no one owns the seabed* or anything on it, which is where matters stood *before* the treaty was written.

That the deep seas are unowned has been the principle underlying freedom of the seas for centuries. A doctrine that seems to proclaim that they are now owned by mankind is used in the treaty to claim the right of an international authority to control and regulate uses of the seas. This theoretical nonsense jeopardizes one of the great foundations of international peace and prosperity—freedom of the high seas.[6]

Not only is the theory wrong, but the factual assumptions underlying the treaty provisions are even more obviously wrong. Some experts probably knew from the beginning that it was all a pipe dream. It was certainly known by many in 1981.[7] In May 1981 spokesmen of the Kennecott Consortium, in a detailed report to the British House of Commons, described how calculations based on surveys in the 1950s and 1960s misled mining companies to think that nodules could become profitable but that "estimates of the total resource of nodules have little significance since they take no account of the economics of recovery," which had been grievously miscalculated. "Only a very small fraction of the total resources of nodules can be classified even as potential reserves—a term that implies that they can be mined profitably." The report contends that the provisions of the treaty are a disincentive for investment in mining but then adds that "even with no legal, economic, or financial restraints a nodule project is unlikely to be in operation before 1990. Market considerations . . . may postpone the first project even longer." Finally, they say, "Whilst it cannot be denied that the total content of manganese, nickel, copper and cobalt in all the nodules in the oceans may be vast, most of this resource will be uneconomic for many decades—*possibly centuries*" (my emphasis).[8]

Two great errors underlying treaty negotiations were that useful minerals were lying there for the taking and that production of the metals from the nodules would be profitable. The reality is that obtaining the nodules would be very costly and hazardous, refining the metals twice as costly as retrieving them, and the prospects for return on investment sufficiently dismal to bring almost all operations to a complete halt. Starting as they did from these two massive errors, the proponents decided that great efforts were justified to regulate the increased activity that would develop—that new courts were needed to judge disputes, that commissions were needed to control production and prices, and that legislative bodies with new principles of representation were needed to ensure that the wealth that would be pouring in would be shared fairly. Dreams of untold wealth are not a new phenomenon in human history, nor are they easy to give up, but in the case of the nodules there is no alternative.

No Market for Seabed Minerals

The chief minerals in the nodules are manganese, copper, nickel, and cobalt. All have been selling at unusually low prices. The nominal price of nickel in early 1983 was the same as in 1974, despite a decade of high inflation. Manganese is used almost entirely in steel production, and steel production is 50 percent or less of plant capacity around the world, with many steel mills closed down, perhaps forever. Not only are cobalt prices low compared with those in recent years (about one-fifth of 1979's all-time high), but the volatility of the price and the uncertainty of supply are encouraging consumers to be wary of using cobalt. The Congressional Budget Office (CBO) issued a study urging a review of cobalt stockpiling.[9] The existing stockpile goal is considerably higher than needed, according to the CBO study; it urged that care be taken not to reduce incentives for development of cobalt substitutes by industry. In short, as *The Economist* wrote of the main ingredient of the deep seabed nodules, "nobody wants these minerals."[10]

Most reports indicate that copper would not be the major factor if there ever were commercial nodule mining, but recent developments in technology make expensive new sources of copper seem even less important commercially. Copper pipe has been replaced by plastics in many applications. Copper wiring is being replaced by fiber optics for much of communications traffic. Not only can this glass product take the place of copper wiring, it will provide a new source of scrap copper to compete with copper from land mines or nodules; one analyst contends that the obsolete copper communications cables will be the biggest new reserve of copper in the world. To add to the indignities being heaped on this splendid metal, once so highly prized and profitable, the U.S. mint now produces annually more than 13 billion pennies that are 97.5 percent zinc (less than half the price of copper), plated with 2.5 percent copper, saving the mint an estimated $25 million a year in metal costs.

Pessimism about the future of many metals seems justified when prices are depressed, but of course those with long experience remind us that prices and profits fluctuate in all commodities and no one can be sure of the future. The prudential rule, partaking of the character of a natural law, is that whatever goes up must come down, for example, petroleum prices in early 1983 after a decade of huge increases. But nothing in nature or experience says that what is down must go up. The example of copper is instructive. The fluctuations are not simply cyclical or the result of the worldwide recession; the causes are in large part technological innovation and substitution and of such a nature that, although unforeseen new uses may be developed, some major uses of copper are unlikely ever to return.

Similar dire prospects exist for steel, and (since over 90 percent of manganese is consumed in the steel industry) as steel goes, so goes manganese. The Ford Motor Company says it is testing an automobile with a body made of plastic described as lighter than aluminum and stronger than most steel. Kyocera Corporation (Kyoto Ceramics) has developed a ceramic diesel automobile engine. It is lightweight, thermal-efficient, and estimated to give a 30 percent reduction in fuel consumption, and it would practically never wear out.[11] Although one cannot know whether it will be put into production, an advance model can be driven now. U.S. Commerce Under Secretary Lionel Olmer has driven it in Japan and is quoted as saying, "It's an experimental model and it idles sort of rough—but it works, that's the main point."

The development of substitutes for metals brings a deep uncertainty that demand, and hence prices, will rise enough (in relation to future prices of everything else) to justify the huge investment costs of retrieving and refining metals from deep seabed nodules. Without a significant growth of demand, mining nodules for profit makes no sense. "Production of metals from nodules now would cost more than from virtually all existing producers and there are still many undeveloped deposits of these metals on land from which they could be produced at lower cost than from nodules."[12]

Irrelevance of the Production Provisions

There has always been an internal contradiction in the mining provisions of the treaty. On the one hand, there was a desire for production and profit, especially for the Enterprise, to produce the revenue to sustain the Authority. On the other hand, there was a powerful tendency to protectionism, to prevent production sufficient to affect the price of minerals from land-mining countries adversely. A major concern was protecting the prices of the metals produced by less-developed land-mining countries heavily dependent on export income, like "the three Zs"—Zaire, Zambia, and Zimbabwe.[13] Canada, too, perhaps alone among the developed nations, was more concerned with devising and enforcing production controls on deep seabed mining than on developing and facilitating the mining. Canada had in mind, of course, its preeminence in nickel mining. Complicated formulas, practically unintelligible even to many experts, were written into the text to empower commissions to regulate production and thereby prices.

In the past few years, however, without any deep seabed mining, prices of these metals have been affected by a combination of factors—worldwide recession, inflated dollars, oil price increases, high interest rates, currency fluctuations, energy conservation measures, discoveries of extensive new land-based mineral reserves, development of substitutes for several metals, and technological advances—unpredicted but powerful in their effects.

In short, the architects of the treaty thought they were designing protections, through production controls, for price stability in commodities. But the kinds of events that happen all the time in the world economy—and that happen with greater intensity and rapidity in our time than ever before in history—were occurring with a complete disregard for the concerns or the powers of the treaty drafters. The forces at work were, in relation to human lawmakers, anarchic; they could not be controlled by anyone's fiat—not by the United Nations, the International Seabed Authority, or solemn words on the heaviest parchment, no matter how many heads of government put their pens to it.

Many proponents of the treaty continue to argue that an international agreement is necessary to give adequate legal security to miners and that without the treaty it will be impossible for them to get financing for mining operations. The fact is that there will be no financing and no investing in deep seabed mining of manganese nodules for profit in the foreseeable future—"possibly centuries"—with or without the treaty. C. R. Tinsley (in 1981 the vice-president,

Mining Division, Continental Bank of Chicago) has written that the treaty's set of mining provisions "brings forth a higher degree of *uncertainty*" (his emphasis) than he had seen in over 250 mining projects worldwide that he had reviewed. His study of the treaty led him to conclude that his bank would not, and probably no bank would, finance deep seabed mining ventures. He added:

> But if a bank is unwilling to "take" or to absorb certain risks, which it traditionally has been able to do in mine project financings all over the world, then we can be safe in anticipating that the companies themselves are not going to take on these risks either.[14]

This view is borne out by the fact that current work and expenditure of the mining groups are negligible and have been for several years now, with no prospect of change.

Some Americans support the seabed provisions for reasons other than profit—for example, for the sake of assured American access to some strategic mineral or the chance to develop new technology. Such activity would probably be limited, and it would surely produce no revenue such as was dreamed of for sharing with the poorer nations. Profitless mining activity will not sustain the Enterprise, nor will it cover the expenses of the Authority and its hoped-for thousands of employees.

Doubts about Practical Purposes

Where does that leave the law of the deep seabed? It was designed to assert ownership over the nodules, set up agencies to license and regulate their retrieval, resolve the anticipated controversies characteristic of a rush for gold or other precious metals, profit from the Enterprise's sale of the metals, and distribute some of the profits to those who need help most. All this was to be done from a headquarters financed from license fees and the rest of the Enterprise's profits, for the grand purpose not merely of producing the revenue to support the entire establishment but especially of taking into its hands, on a supranational basis, the task of aiding the developing world. The aim was to take a giant step in the direction of a new international economic order.

None of these expectations was justified, and none will come to pass. For the foreseeable future there will be no financing (with or without the treaty), no investing, no mining, no licenses, no fees, no disputes to settle, and no contributions from the United States (and no assurance of participation from most of the other nations with a deep seabed mining capability). Thus there is no prospect of funds for the Authority, the courts, the expert commissions, or the secretariat, no technology or capital to transfer to the Enterprise, and no revenue to share with the poorest countries.

If I am right (and I will later consider objections to the argument presented here), a question arises that goes beyond the details of metals and their markets. Why did the proponents of the treaty persist in trying to have it signed and ratified? That is, if the expected activities were not going to occur, why did they continue the effort to generate new agencies to guide and control them? If there was going to be little or no production, why did they persist in establishing means to control production? If the activity was going to be so limited and the likelihood of disputes so remote, why did they try to establish specialized new international courts to adjudicate? If there was going to be no revenue, why did they continue with plans for an expensive establishment that would equal the United Nations itself? Why, when there is no practical purpose to serve, did the proponents of the treaty persist?

Unkind answers come immediately to mind. One is that the treaty negotiators had spent a decade and more in a tight world of their own (a world of their own making, one might say) and could not bear to see it fall short of realization. It would not be the first time that negotiators have become so committed to their own handiwork that they lost touch with the interests of their countries (especially when the matter is of so little interest, as in this case, that few governments have more than a handful of persons, even in the foreign ministry, who know or care anything about the treaty).

Another unkind explanation is concern about careers: many of the diplomats have devoted a major part of their professional careers to the law of the sea. Some of the younger ones have never done anything else. It is *their* subject, their expertise; if the treaty organization does not come into being, they have no way of knowing what other assignment may ever come to them. A test of the validity of this explanation would be to propose one brief addition to the text of the treaty: that no one who has participated in its writing may hold any position of trust in the Authority or the Enterprise or any of its agencies. It is unlikely that such a provision would receive support, but if by some magic it were made a part of the text, support for the treaty would decline sharply among the diplomats. This explanation, I repeat, is unkind and surely not the basic factor. Nevertheless, diplomats would have to be inhuman for it to be of no significance whatsoever.

An explanation of a different sort is more convincing, the one I

COMMON SENSE VERSUS COMMON HERITAGE

started with—ideology. Serious professionals who care about the work they do, who are devoted to the principles that guide them and the causes they live for—and that is a fair and accurate description of the proponents of the treaty—do not expend great effort aimlessly. They worked unbelievably hard and very skillfully for a decade to produce the most complex international agreement ever devised. Along the way conditions either changed or emerged from obscurity to visibility only gradually. In any case, at some time—sooner for some than for others—all the competent ones saw that the facts were not as initially described and that expectations were not going to be fulfilled.

In the face of these changes they agreed to some adjustments but never to any basic ones. They never looked for the elegant reformulations that astute and proud professionals would make if they wished to. When it became clear, for example, that the production-level formulas no longer made sense, they made a "concession" to the United States by changing the formula so that it would have "no bite," but they would not even consider giving up the power to set production levels, nor would they eliminate the commission to exercise that power.

Again, they were willing to make a "concession" that had the practical effect of nullifying the mandatory character of the transfer of technology—but a suggestion that the word "mandatory" be deleted brought only amused smiles that said, in effect, there are some things more important than technology, and the word "mandatory," with all it implies, is one of them.

Again, the text of the treaty provides that the assembly (not the council) be the supreme body. Proponents sought to reassure by arguing that many provisions taken together demonstrate that the assembly (dominated by third world countries, because they are so numerous) would not really be, for practical purposes, supreme, but suggestions that the text be reworded to accord with their reading of it were not taken seriously.

What can the explanation be for insisting on going forward when no practical purpose would be served? Why, if some provisions for the deep seabed must remain in the text, did the conference refuse to make revisions to delete unnecessary powers and agencies? The answer is ideology, the ideology of "the common heritage of mankind," the single most sacred of UN sacred cows. If one were to suggest that the deep seabed provisions now be deleted from the treaty, that the remainder—the true law of the sea treaty—be presented for signature and ratification and put into effect, and that the question of the law of the deep seabed be approached separately and anew on the basis of what is now known, such a proposal would receive the same response as recommendations that India increase its food supply by slaughtering and eating cows, and for a similar reason.[15]

"Common Heritage" versus Common Sense

If there were no ideological barrier, if the law of the deep seabed could be approached now on the basis of common sense instead of "the common heritage of mankind" ideology, we could quickly agree on several things. First, we could agree that there is enough time to proceed sensibly; there is no rush and no crisis. Second, not much, if anything, in the way of new international structures or agencies is required. The activity related to the deep seabed will be far less than the activity on the seas, and the agencies and regulatory efforts should be minimal, commensurate with the low level of activity. The private mining consortia have already met; in a very short time they came to an agreement on procedures, by negotiation or arbitration, to settle any disputes that might arise over mining sites. Probably some simple system for registering claims for sites could handle all the necessary work, since it is estimated that in all international waters there will be no more than five to twenty sites for mining nodules for the foreseeable future. Most important, there should be no claim put forth of an *inherent right* of an international authority to regulate deep seabed activities.

One of the most fervent proponents of "the common heritage of mankind" doctrine, Elisabeth Mann Borgese, a leader of the world government movement in the years after World War II (until that movement for global harmony destroyed itself by internal strife among rival world federalist factions), agrees that ideology is the dominant factor. After listing some developments that have diminished "the value of the Common Heritage of Mankind, particularly of the manganese nodules," she goes on to say that that is not the main point. The main point is that "the creation of the International Seabed Authority . . . must be reckoned as a breakthrough in international relations. Here is an international institution," she writes,

> unprecedentedly empowered to regulate and act on the basis of the new principle of the Common Heritage of Mankind. Here is a first attempt at a global production policy with due regard to conservation of the environment. Here is an opening to industrial cooperation between the North and the South based not on aid but on sharing. . . . The International

144

Seabed Authority, a utopian dream of 20 years ago, is now a fact of international law. Something has been moving.[16]

What clearer evidence can there be that for many proponents of the treaty, ideology takes precedence over the explicit practical goals? If one were to protest that Mrs. Borgese, no matter how devoted and enthusiastic, does not speak for all treaty proponents, we are still left with the puzzle: why, when the stated practical reasons for going forward with the law of the deep seabed have all dissolved, do the advocates nevertheless persist? My answer is that the ideology of "the common heritage" is, as Mrs. Borgese tells us, of overriding importance.[17]

Reasonably Facing the Unforeseeable

I am aware that others might say my analysis is factually wrong, that there are indeed untold riches out there, if not nodules then something else, and that some form of mining or other activities foreseen or unforeseen will indeed occur. Let me turn, then, to these objections.

The very experience I have described teaches that we cannot know what the future will reveal. New discoveries are being made now—for instance, deposits of polymetallic sulfides containing metals in much higher concentrations than the nodules—and it is considered a certainty that more and richer deposits of nonliving materials will be found in unexpected places and forms not limited to metals. Proponents of the treaty say that for this reason we must be prepared with agencies and regulations to ensure an orderly, peaceful, and fair exploitation of the sea's riches, whatever they turn out to be. Without a legal structure, they say, there will be chaos or paralysis: either every claim an occasion for strife and even violence or no exploitation at all because those who might be active would be intimidated by the uncertainty and danger of an anarchic situation. These, I admit, are valid and formidable objections—but they are answerable.

The attempt to establish elaborate systems and formulas to deal with every detail of the future turned out to be an extravagant waste of time and human talent. The structure was static, and the subject matter was fluid. Sensible (rather than doctrinaire) action to bring order to the extraction of raw materials from international waters may be based on several guiding principles:

• Use existing international agencies, which are numerous enough already, rather than generate new ones.
• Let the regulatory forces be commensurate with the activities to be regulated.

145

- Insist on the principle of encouraging discovery and extraction of materials useful to all, rather than discouraging them.
- Encourage nations to cooperate, without unnecessary and complicated international agency interference.
- If nongovernment, for-profit corporations are the ones capable of exploration and extraction, encourage them to function according to their nature and capabilities.
- Assert and impose on others no doctrines that are not necessary for the immediate task (that is, eschew imperious globalism and sweeping claims to powers that are potentially tyrannical).

In short, as an opponent of the provisions dealing with the deep seabed and as a proponent of the provisions dealing with the sea, I urge that steps be taken now to make a fresh start. Let the deep seabed provisions be deleted from the text—Authority, Enterprise, and all. The United States would not delay in signing what would be left: a true law of the sea treaty. The two parts are not naturally linked and are severable; there is no reason why one part should be held hostage to the other. Deliberations could then begin to make simple and brief rules, when any are needed, commensurate with the activity at the time, using existing entities, aiming to encourage activity, and adding provisions as they might be found necessary.

Provision could be made that a share of profits go to those less fortunate, but to make that possible the rules must be such that profit making is not only permitted but encouraged. A small office with a dozen or so workers could be established to register claims and to keep records of disputes and their resolution through negotiation or arbitration.

The True Meaning of "Common Heritage"

What of "the common heritage of mankind"? Can it have no place in new deliberations? My opinion is that a deep seabed treaty is not needed now. When one is needed, if the common heritage theme is reintroduced, let us hope that this time, for the first time, it would be considered as seriously and as respectfully as it deserves. It would be a service to rescue the common heritage of mankind from the abuse it has suffered at the hands of its ideologues.

The word "heritage" has at least two meanings, one referring to material possessions that are heritable, the other to immaterial principles of good, civilizing truths and wisdom that are handed down from age to age, as expressed in phrases such as "the heritage of constitutional liberty."

Although it would be difficult if not impossible to explain just what sequence of steps led to the false conclusion that all of us have "inherited" the manganese nodules at the bottom of the sea, that meaning of heritage—the material inheritance of property—seems to have dominated the treaty negotiations. This is especially ironic because the initial intention, no doubt, was to elevate our thoughts about the human condition, to encourage us to regard all human beings as equally deserving of treatment as one "kind."

Instead, very quickly, enthusiasts were speaking of metals as the common heritage, the area to be brought under control of the Authority as "the common heritage area," and the revenue that would flow in as "common heritage dollars." Even today, so high-minded a person as Mrs. Borgese worries about the decline of "the value of the Common Heritage of Mankind, particularly of the manganese nodules." One can see *how* it happened. But *why* do intelligent and principled people collaborate in the debasement of such a splendid phrase and allow thought polluters to give ugly little rocks lying in the darkest depths of all creation the noble title of mankind's common heritage? Even if the nodules were pure gold, such usage would be desecration.

Mankind's true heritage lies in the great human accomplishments. I mean books, music, plays, paintings, sculptures, buildings; I mean the search for the truth of things through philosophy, theology, poetry, physics, astronomy, mathematics, logic—yes, even rhetoric. This is not the place to attempt to describe it, but there is a connection, even a progression, from philosophy (seeking knowledge of the nature of things) to technology (the power to use knowledge to transform nature to improve the human condition). Sever the bond, separate philosophy and technology, and we are left with a defective "heritage," either formless *stuff* or airy abstraction.

Human beings are not capable of "creation," the divine power to make something out of nothing. We are bound to materials; that is why we explore ceaselessly to find them. But one aspect of the best in mankind, what is often called the divine within us, is the striving to make much out of little, progressively making more and more out of less and less. Sometimes the most advanced technology is spoken of as "miraculous," by which we mean that in the mixture of mind and matter, the matter is so lowly and the quantity of it so negligible (for example, silicon chips from sand) that the combined product is almost immaterial, almost all mind, as if divinely made, just as we tend to call the best poetry or music "heavenly."

If most practical-minded diplomats would consider this a strange approach to useful thinking about the deep seabed, they would be right. But we must not forget that *they* are the ones who introduced "the common heritage of mankind" into the proceedings and never ceased to brandish it thereafter. Their failure to understand what they were talking about explains, at least in part, why a decade of their brilliant work has ended in contention, bitterness, and failure. In my opinion nothing could be more practical than to reflect on the two different meanings of the heritage and to instill into the proceedings, should there be more of them, some of the higher meaning of the word. Let those who are unwilling or unable to rise to that level acknowledge, honestly, that they were never really serious when they used the phrase, and then let them get on with the job without singing anthems to the common heritage of mankind.

What good might come from serious reflection in treaty deliberations on the human heritage? It might remind us that raw materials, whether low-grade ore or high-grade petroleum, are valuable only if we know what to do with them. Raw materials *in themselves* are worthless. The ability to reason and imagine, to learn what to do with raw materials, is what is common to us all, is what makes us, equally, all of one kind. The only true resources are human understanding and the ability to make nature serviceable.

The great error of the treaty negotiators was to speak and think of the *nodules* as the common heritage of mankind and to ignore—worse, to shackle—the true heritage all human beings share, the rational power to make the most of what nature gives, for the betterment of all.

PART FIVE

Liberal Education—
Doubting Mother, Country, God

14
Prescription for Suppressing a Dreadful Thought

I commence by posing four questions that have been in the back of my mind, and probably yours, bothering and perplexing us, for years, perhaps for decades.

• Why are the families of students seen on liberal arts college campuses at commencement but not at other times?

• Why does liberal education alienate students from their families?

• Why do liberal arts students tend to behave in uncivil—in fact, uncivilized—ways toward family, community, and tradition?

• Why will the graduates, a few years from now as alumni, complain about the students' lack of respect for family, community, and tradition?

It may be rash to say so, but my purpose is to enable you to perceive the answers to these baffling questions.

I first started hearing commencement addresses thirty years ago and have had to listen to many since. Some have been bad, some better. The first one I heard, in 1947, was memorable. The familiar opening of commencement speeches goes something like this: "As I look at your bright and shining faces, my heart fills with hope for the future, for you are about to step forth to become the leaders of a better tomorrow." The speech I remember, back in 1947, was very different. It began: "As I look at you, the first class to graduate since the end of the war, I cannot suppress a dreadful thought." The "dreadful thought" was that these graduates had not been prepared for life by their college studies, and very properly so; the reason given was that a college is a community ruled by reason and the world is mad. A good college should not prepare students to live a life of madness.

Since that commencement day I have had enough experience of the world and of colleges to form my own judgment that college communities are not as reasonable and the world is not as mad as the speaker thought. Yet I agree with his conclusion: the best college education does not prepare you for life; further, the best college education should not prepare you for life. Let me explain why I think so.

Each of us is one being, whole and complete, a person, an individual. Each of us is also a part of some larger entity—family, community, town or city, nation—in some way incomplete except as one part of a larger human whole.

Despite this duality of being one separate individual and also a part of a larger whole, we know of societies, usually primitive, in which the community sense is so overwhelming that its members have no sense of individuality or even of existence separate from the community. It is probable that long ago just about all communities were like that.

How then did a sense of individuality originate? Perhaps as a result of travel or, rather, the tales of travelers returning to tell how differently people lived and thought in distant places. The fascination must have been great at those first reports of peoples who did not do things "our way."

Travelers' stories led to the question, eventually, Is our way better than their way? From there it is not many steps to the question that signals the beginning of philosophy, Is there a *best* way? The pursuit of the answer to that question requires a significant degree of liberation from the domination of the community, liberation from unquestioning conformity to "our way." Once that question is asked, the individual separated from community asserts itself.

Colleges of liberal education are the arenas—sometimes the battleground—for the struggle for the emergence of those who have the character to ask questions and search for answers that put them very much on their own, individuals who can cut themselves off, lonely seekers who are willing to ask the question, How do I know that our way is the best way? and who are prepared to suffer the consequences. To ask that question is to loosen or cut the ties that bind in a thousand ways, for looking for the best way leads to questioning everything—motherhood, patriotism, religion, everything. Let me give you some examples.

When I was a college freshman, we were discussing *Oedipus Rex* in a seminar. We were all horrified, as one must be, by the crime of Oedipus, who killed his father and married his mother, unknowingly, but nevertheless. . . . One classmate stunned us all by asking, "What's so terrible about killing your father and marrying your mother? How is it worse than killing any older man and marrying his widow?" That question, one can see at once, is appropriate (though shocking) in a classroom seminar. Once it is asked, a serious effort must be made to discuss it. But it takes no argument to assert that such a question is certainly not appropriate in polite society. To put it simply, there are obvious obstacles to its serious consideration at the family dinner table.

Consider, as another example, the Declaration of Independence. There are all sorts of situations when good Americans affirm their wholehearted acceptance of the truths that all men are created equal and endowed with unalienable rights; but in a good college, affirmation will not do; there must be questioning. Are such "truths" "self-evident"? Are men equal? Do we have a "right" to liberty, let alone the pursuit of happiness? No liberal arts college is true to its purpose that does not ask these questions in all seriousness. But as a citizen in public discourse it is an entirely different matter to raise such doubts by asking such questions. Community is not strengthened by challenges to its basic premises and principles.

Consider one more example. When one studies religion, or religions, in a good liberal arts college, the question unavoidably arises of the existence of God. The question may be raised by the most eminent authority, say Thomas Aquinas; but once it is raised, there is no guarantee what the outcome will be for any one student. A good liberal arts college trains students not to accept arguments on the word of an authority. A student may very well study Thomas's proof of the existence of God and come to his own conclusion that God does not exist. Whether God exists, with the answer seriously in doubt, is not the sort of question and answer it is prudent to indulge in just any place around town, certainly not in most taverns. But it is an obligation of a liberal arts college to provide the setting for such questioning and for the possibility of such an answer.

The liberal arts college and liberal arts students must question Mother, Country, and God, and in so doing they necessarily observe their own society as outsiders would, free of the preconceptions that bind the community together. Serious students make themselves outsiders, strangers, aliens to their native community.

Further, as detached observers and inquirers, they notice how much partisanship distorts what other people say and even what they see. Unquestioning allegiance to the ways of our own community blind us to many ideas and events that are visible to those who are not bound. This makes students feel superior, partly justifiably. Students are, in a way, inferior to others: they are students for the very reason that they lack knowledge that others can impart to them. In another way, however, students can be superior to nonstudents: they know that they do not know and are thus superior to those who also do not know but do not know that they do not know.

The self-imposed separation of students from their own community reminds us of Aristotle's teaching that one who is not part of the *polis*, not part of the political community, is not a human being but something lower or higher, either a beast or a god. That students are often bestial in their behavior is such a commonplace as to require no further explanation. But that students are also often godlike needs a lot of explaining. How else, however, can we describe beings who are expected to spend their time contemplating the meanings of time and eternity; space and infinity; the order of the universe; magnitude, measure, and number; and questions such as what life is and what nature is?

When we say of a student that "she is lost in thought" or that "he is in another world," we are describing a godlike being, not part of our *polis*, not here with us in town, not a fellow citizen in the proper sense. At such moments, which may be rare even for the best students, all their energy is concentrated in activity that is independent of other persons and connections. No interests, no loyalties, no responsibilities mar the effort to understand, to know, to see, to grasp the truth. The young person senses that in that very effort, as briefly as it may be sustained, there is a triumph and a glorying and an elevation, an experience of what it is to share in divinity—whether understood in the Greek way or an earlier or a later way.

Socrates is the exemplar of what I have been describing. He lived the questioning life. He was the one most fully realized, complete, and independent mind and soul—and he did it by questioning everything. So it is only fitting that I reveal to you that he is the one who contradicted most emphatically the argument I have been making. According to Plato, a day or two before the execution of Socrates, his friend Crito came to him in his prison cell and told him that he had bribed the guards and arranged for Socrates to escape to safety in exile. Socrates replied that he would not break the law and harm his own city even to save his life, because he was, after all, the child and the slave of the laws. The city and the laws, Socrates said, gave him his life. He was fully theirs, and he had no right to disobey the laws even though the citizens had convicted and condemned him unjustly.

Even if we allow for the exaggeration in this argument (it is an exaggeration, of course, for no one known to us in history or literature was more his own man and owed less to others for what he was than Socrates), even if we deny that any person is a slave to the political community, still we fool ourselves if we think that any of us achieves anything of significance without the help of others, independent of the support of family, friends, relatives, fellow citizens, and even strangers.

While all of you, however briefly, were truly students—I mean at those transcendent moments when you were *truly* lost in *real* thought—you were being fed, housed, clothed, and taught by the strenuous efforts and genuine sacrifices of parents, professors, citizens of this state and of the entire United States who pay taxes, donors to the college, and utter strangers who, for one reason and another, contributed. Thousands of fellow members of dozens of communities banded together, as if you were fully one of them, to take care of you, to nurture you, to tolerate and help you, even if they could not love you or even understand you.

Although it was your student's duty to the search for truth to be godlike and unfettered and independent, it was never really possible. You are bound, and will be bound, to dozens, and scores, and hundreds, and thousands, and millions, and billions of other human beings, with ties that cannot be cut or broken or dissolved.

You were never free as a god. You were never even as free as a bird.

You were and will always be a combination of independent individual and community-bound citizen: on the one hand, one on whom no one may make a claim, living and thinking only for yourself, isolated, solitary, responsible only to yourself and to the standards of the arts; on the other hand, a citizen caught up in all the responsibilities and obligations of a member of society.

That combination of separateness and belonging is the fact of life for all of us, students and nonstudents. We cannot be rid of one or the other. Only the balance of emphasis can be changed. While you were an undergraduate, the highest duty of the college was to emphasize independence, to teach you how to think for yourself, to assign to you tasks that had to be carried out without help from, or even regard for, others. The aim was to help you realize your own powers, to bring to their fullest development those human resources that are yours alone and that no one can share with you or develop for you. Your duty to the college and to yourself was to think your own thoughts and to be, as much as possible, your own man, your own woman.

Now the emphasis necessarily switches. Now you rejoin the outside community and must begin again to share yourself with others in countless varied and responsible ways. Although you have (everyone has) a natural aptitude for it and although you already have plenty of experience of it (everyone has), the college did not prepare you for that sharing. But there is no real cause for concern or anxiety. You will learn—some easily and quickly, others more slowly and painfully, but all in good time—how to be a good, solid, responsible, contributing, sharing member of one and another community, from the family to the world.

155

As you become more fully a community person, you owe it to this college, and to the spirit of liberal education, and to yourself, and to that grand community sometimes called the Republic of Letters, to hold back something of yourself—not to neglect and thus lose those powers developed here at such great effort and price; to think your own thoughts; to be your own private person; to remember your share of divinity, potential in every human being, actual in those who struggle to nurture it. Be aware that inside your head, in the vast and fascinating reaches of a disciplined mind and imagination, there are other worlds to dwell in, and explore, and improve.

15
Learning to Earn a Living and Learning to Live a Life

The *Oxford English Dictionary* tells us that in the fourteenth century the word "commencement" was being used to describe "the great ceremony" at which degrees were conferred at Cambridge University. People who were candidates for degrees were often referred to as "commencers," and, when there was a deliberation about whether to accept a student as a candidate for a degree, the question was whether he was "commenceable."

If we think about it, it is a very strange name for a ceremony that marks a successful ending, a completion. Why then should it be called a commencement? When we say commencement, we seem to give no acknowledgment to the tremendous accomplishment we should be celebrating.

Four years ago there were 220 entering freshmen in this college. Today there are 117 graduates. Many start and not very many finish. It takes hard work, hard study. For many of you there has been tremendous sacrifice, on your part and on your family's part. Through it all, with all the challenges and difficulties, you have steadily worked your way through very demanding requirements. In four years you have learned more than most people in the world ever know. In truth, you have learned more than you know.

Why then is this called commencement? Why not something more complimentary? Why not call it achievement day? or fulfillment day? or day of the survivors? or day of the winners? "Commencement" does not say any of that. "Commencement" does not even give a nod to what you have accomplished. "Commencement" seems to reduce you to the rank of beginner, someone just starting, a commencer. It seems, curtly and coldly, to say, "All right, you, back to the starting line." It seems to say, "You think you're so smart; you think you're something special. Well, we have news for you. As far as we are concerned, you're nothing but a beginner."

My news for you is that as harsh as that sounds, the facts are that you go to the commencing line with tremendous advantages. Everyone hears about how hard it is for young college graduates to get a start, and no doubt the beginning can be difficult for many. But consider, first, your skills. You have some specific skills, your major: social service or social science or political science or art education or psychology or sociology; and you also have some general skills, or liberal skills as I prefer to call them, or liberal arts, as they are commonly called. I mean such trained and developed and practiced skills as reasoning, reckoning, writing, speaking, listening, analyzing, synthesizing, experimenting, translating, and—perhaps the most important skill of all—learning how to learn. Those are formidable skills, very salable in the job market.

Spokesmen for vocational or career education speak often of salable skills and the duty of schools to provide them. I agree. No one should be allowed to leave school without salable skills. Teaching salable skills is a duty of every school. But in what I have just said there is a profound problem. Which skills are salable? Which skills are most reliably salable?

There is a difficulty in trying to prepare for particular jobs in a free society. The problem is that the market keeps changing its mind about which specific jobs it needs to fill this season or this year. Examples abound of the difficulty. Home construction, for instance. For those who are trained to build homes, in some years there is no demand for their skills, and in other years they cannot keep up with the demand.

Consider teaching. Twenty or twenty-five years ago the federal government and other governments were forming commissions to try to figure out how to train enough teachers to meet the demand. There were never enough. Now, of course, many of those commissions still exist, because commissions never die, but the need for them has certainly gone, and the big problem now is retrenchment: how to find other appropriate work for persons trained to be schoolteachers.

Consider watchmaking. All over the world people have been trained to make and repair watches. Now there are quartz watches with no moving parts. What will happen to those people who have the old watchmaking skill and only that skill?

Consider slide rules. You used to see slide rules by the thousands on campuses all over the country. Now you never see one because of electronic calculators. What has happened to the people who were trained in that and only that salable skill—that one salable skill—of making slide rules? There is no demand for their training, however skillful they may have been.

In a free society, with a relatively free market, there is a high degree of uncertainty when it comes to selling skills. How bad is uncertainty? Uncertainty is something like old age. It is terrible except compared with the alternative. The alternative to uncertainty in the job market is certainty; and what do you have to do to achieve certainty in the job market? The price of certainty is being told to pack up and go where someone else decides you are needed to fill a job. There is no uncertainty in societies where the government dictates what will be studied, to fill what jobs, where, and by whom.

Some years ago I visited the Soviet Union with a group of educators, visiting universities and other kinds of schools. A lot of official information was provided, of course, but the most enlightening session I had was an unofficial discussion with some medical students about to graduate. They were in despair because every one of them had more certainty than he or she wanted. Each knew where he or she was going to be sent, to which small Siberian town, to fill the vacancy the government had decided had to be filled. They would have welcomed the uncertainty some of you may face because they would have been delighted, thrilled, with the freedom of choice implicit in that uncertainty.

Even if some uncertainty is preferable to certainty, too much uncertainty is no pleasure. Just how uncertain is your future? I hope you know that you have already been given, and have given yourself, a tremendous advantage at the "commencing" line. Unemployment statistics for workers with different levels of schooling show just how much difference schooling makes. (Notice I will be speaking about "schooling," not "education," because the statistics are based on the number of years attended in a school. They do not tell what you studied, how much you learned, how well you did it. But consider how much difference schooling makes)

My figures are for March 1975, a very bad time, the worst month for unemployment in your lifetime. Unemployment stood over 9 percent, the highest figure since the Great Depression, and that 9 percent was for all workers in the labor force. But unemployment for young workers, under twenty-five, was much worse, almost double; 17 percent of them were unemployed. And those under twenty-five who had not finished high school were in an even worse situation; their unemployment was 25 percent. But here is the startling and heartening news for you: in that same worst month, in that same age group, under twenty-five, those who had four years of college study had an unemployment rate of just 6 percent.

You often hear about the problem of the relation of study and work, that study programs must be revised because they do not prepare young people for work. It is very clear to me that that is not the problem. The big problem is the relation of nonstudy and work.

159

The young people who have not finished high school have four times as high an unemployment rate as those who have four years of college.

As impressive as that low 6 percent is, in the worst month ever, for young college-trained workers, the news gets even better as they get older. When unemployment for all workers was over 9 percent, for graduates between the ages of twenty-five and fifty-five it was only 2½ percent, and for graduates who were over fifty-five, it was just 1.7 percent.

Thus even at the worst times, in the few years before you reach the age of twenty-five, you have about 94 chances out of 100 to find a job. You have already beaten much tougher odds than that. You had only about 53 chances in 100 to be sitting here today as a graduate when you started as a freshman. In this warm, friendly, cloistered world, the odds you have beaten were almost twice as tough as you will ever again encounter in that cold, unfriendly outside world.

Let me try to read the mind of at least one skeptic among you. And if you have not become somewhat skeptical in four years of education, you have not been doing your homework. A skeptic would say, "Sure, I'll find a job. But what kind of job? What is this man Goldwin trying to put over on us? Is he trying to peddle good news to us? Doesn't he know that we know that if it isn't bad news it isn't true? We know about the kinds of jobs this dreary, vulgar, commercial, debased, bourgeois society condemns us to. We know that most people live lives of quiet desperation and find no joy in their work. Those are the jobs he is trying to talk us into," the skeptic says, "and we want none of it."

The trouble with many of our notions about jobs and job satisfaction is that they are based on anecdotal evidence and sources such as movies, novels, and human interest news reporting—and for their purposes, happy, satisfied people are not very useful or interesting. But when real working people are asked whether they are satisfied with their jobs, an overwhelming proportion of American workers, well over 90 percent, say that, yes, indeed, they are satisfied with their jobs. This is a longstanding and consistent fact. It has been going on unabated for years. Survey after survey of people in every kind of occupation shows that between 1958 and 1973 there was no discernible decline in job satisfaction among workers as a whole, among college-educated workers, or among young people. This was so even throughout the 1960s, when one would have expected people to be alienated and dissatisfied. Year after year studies show that job satisfaction remains well over 90 percent.

Furthermore, in studies of thousands of college graduates ten or fifteen years after commencement, so few answer that they are "not at all satisfied" with their jobs, just 4 percent, that the only real distinction is between those who say they are "very satisfied" and those who say they are "somewhat satisfied"—and many more say they are "very satisfied" than "somewhat satisfied."

I do not want to drown you in the survey data, but just let me add a few facts, because they are so contrary to prevailing misconceptions and also because they are good news for those of you who may need some encouragement:

• College graduates, ten or fifteen years later, report that the range of good jobs was much broader than was visible to them as students.

• Income goes higher, and job satisfaction increases sharply, at successive levels of years of schooling.

• Graduates who say they do not use their college major in their work are about as satisfied with their jobs as those who say they do use their major on the job, and their incomes are about the same.

• Graduates change jobs and line of work often in the first few years. About ten years out of college they have job and career stability. The lesson is that if you want to know how well graduates do and what they do, it is a good idea to wait ten years before you ask.

• Younger workers (under twenty-five) are less satisfied than older workers—so the young ones are not the best source of information on what working life will be like in the long run.

• Salary is not the whole story. Many graduates who say that they are not well paid say, nevertheless, that they are very satisfied with their work.

• More than half of graduates surveyed fifteen years later report that they chose their current occupation after college. They did not prepare for it specifically in college. But whether they chose early or late had no effect on job satisfaction.

There is a lesson in that to educators, to guidance counselors, and to parents. You cannot be sure you are right in advising young people to choose a career early if they are unsure themselves what to spend their lives on. Any graduate has a good chance to be satisfied in his work whenever he makes his career choice. His chances of success are just as great whether he decides late or early.

All my talk about your newly acquired material advantages might be called "the dollar argument" for higher education. I hope it satisfies anyone who thinks that education must bring a material reward to justify its high cost in money, time, and effort. But it does not satisfy me, and it should not satisfy you. Advocates of liberal arts studies are fond of saying that the highest goal of education is not learning to earn a living but learning to live a life. Yet they go on to fall into their own trap by arguing that higher education helps you to better jobs and higher earnings, as if that payoff were its highest purpose. Let us not make that mistake.

If that were my whole message to you, the implication would be insulting to you and to your families and to the college. It would imply that your interest in study was wholly selfish and material, entirely in the spirit of "what's in it for me?" I don't believe that about you, and I do not believe your elders and your teachers want you to be that way, however much they may wish for your material success.

One high purpose of the kind of liberal education you have had is to liberate you from narrowness, to make you more aware of yourself and what it means to be a human being, to add to your understanding of what human beings are like in their fundamental nature, and thus to make you more aware of the rest of society and the rest of the world. Liberal education serves to open your eyes to the needs of others and your responsibility toward them.

After all, as hard as you have worked and as much as you and your families may have sacrificed, you are not self-educated. You have had secret benefactors. Many other people have contributed to make your education possible, some you do not even know and who do not know you. Not one of you has paid the full cost of his education. No one pays the full cost of his education, here or in any college. Society as a whole has paid a sizable share. Society as a whole has invested in you. It has paid out in advance. It is relying on you. And you owe it.

You owe a debt you can never finish repaying—and now I am not speaking only or even primarily of a debt that can be repaid in money—those are the easy ones. Debts of faith and trust are the hard ones to repay. But I will not exhort you. I do not believe that exhortation is effective or appropriate in these times. I will instead assert some obvious facts:

• It is a fact that the world always has too much of injustice, cowardice, selfishness, hatred, misery, discord, and fear.

• It is a fact that we always have too much ugliness and too few makers of beauty, too much ignorance and too few teachers of truth, too much hunger and want and too few real producers.

• It is a fact that the world never has enough men and women who are loving, decent, considerate, courageous, productive, moderate, humane, gentle, and strong.

• It is a fact that these finest qualities, and the men and women who embody them, are always in short supply—desperately short supply.

From these stark facts I leave you to draw your own conclusions about what you must repay: what you owe to your education, to your teachers, to your family, to your community, to your nation, to humanity, and to yourself. An answer in words will not suffice. Your answer must be expressed in deeds, in a lifetime of deeds. That process of answering is what commences today.

16
The Future of Liberal Education

I have three kinds of news to deliver about the future of liberal education: bad news, worse news, and good news.

First, the bad news: liberal education is in danger; its future is precarious at best. The United States is, above all else, a nation of very practical-minded people. If we spend time and money and effort, we want a return. We like to know quite specifically what we are buying. It is easy to estimate the value of a course on how to upholster a chair or how to repair an automobile, easy to judge what price makes it worth our while for a vocation as an upholsterer or an auto mechanic or for a do-it-yourself hobby.

But how do we know how much money or time is a good investment to study Victorian literature or ancient and modern theories of political society? We might be convinced that such things are important, but how do we put a price on them? As every salesperson—and every consumer—knows, when the price is in doubt, the sale is in doubt.

Some people say that price is not a problem because so many courses are now available free or for a very low tuition charge. But, of course, there is no such thing as a free service. Courses offered in public institutions or in some private institutions may cost the user relatively little or even nothing, but that just means the service is subsidized by others, either by donors or by taxpayers, which means that it is paid for at full cost but in a different way. And there is no way for others to subsidize the student's cost in personal effort.

So the question remains, What is important enough to teach and to study at considerable cost to individuals or to society as a whole? Is liberal education part of what is important? Liberal education is in a precarious position in these times because the answer to the latter question is not obviously and automatically yes; the answer takes some thinking about.

Annoyance

The future of liberal education is precarious. That is the bad news. The second kind of news is worse: liberal education has always been in danger, has always been in a precarious situation. The primary reason can be stated briefly and bluntly: it is part of the nature of liberal education that it is annoying and the people who are liberally educated are annoying. They may be helpful, they may provide beauty and joy to our lives, they may even be absolutely indispensable, but above all they are annoying; they are truly a public nuisance.

The aim of liberal education is to know the truth, and the activity of liberal education is to ask unsettling questions. Liberal education questions what society does not question; it challenges beliefs that society accepts as true; it insists that things that are obscure, complicated, difficult, and even dreary are really more deserving of our attention than things that are clear, simple, easy, and immediately entertaining. What could be more annoying?

Liberal education also claims to know what is good for us. In fact, it claims to know better than we know ourselves what is good for us. We keep asking, if it is so good for us, why does it so often bore us and fatigue us and make us feel like rebellious children waiting for the school bell to ring?

Not just in twentieth-century America but in all times and societies, it has been hard to see just what we can do with a liberal education—just how we can make a living with it. Long ago a liberally educated man wrote that "to a starving man, bread is more important than philosophy." At what financial distance from starvation does the balance start to shift away from bread to philosophy? The liberally educated are often seen waiting at the doors of the rich and powerful, but how often are the rich and powerful seen waiting at the doors of the liberally educated?

Legitimate doubts, annoyances, and complaints endanger liberal education, now and in all times, and make its future precarious, inevitably. Liberal education can thrive only with strong support from the public or from powerful patrons, and why should we expect such support for what is considered a public nuisance and even a threat to those who are powerful?

If anyone doubts the annoyance power of liberal studies and the people who make such studies a full-time occupation, if anyone thinks I am exaggerating, just remember ancient Athens and Socrates.

Socrates was the glory of Athens—in my opinion more so than its poets, its playwrights, its sculptors, its architects, its political leaders—and Athens was the best city in the ancient world, perhaps the best ever. What authority do I have for that last claim? Socrates himself. He never left Athens except in military service. Even when death was the alternative, Socrates refused an offer to leave Athens to live elsewhere. But the Athenians executed Socrates for the crime of annoyance—extreme, upsetting, aggravated annoyance. What annoyed them? His complete dedication to thinking and questioning and seeking the truth. He questioned everything, and that was intolerable. If ancient Athens did not tolerate the finest example of the liberally educated man, what kind of society will be hospitable to those who try to follow his example? The obvious answer to that question explains why I say that liberal education is and always has been and probably always will be in danger.

Liberated Psyches

I have talked all this time about liberal education without defining my terms. It is not easy for me to be as precise as others might be, because I am not one who thinks of liberal education primarily as certain courses or subjects.

It is much easier for others, who think liberal education is a certain list of subjects, to tell you what liberal education is. English literature is, for example, and carpentry is not. "I teach the liberal arts," someone says, and we guess, Is it philosophy, poetry, history, languages, literature, theology, or some interdisciplinary combination of them? We know it is not carpentry: too practical. We are not sure that physics or biology should be included; we are not sure that sciences are part of liberal education: they have a fairly direct practical use, after all.

When I speak of liberal education, I do not start by thinking of certain subjects or authors or books, although I may end that way, as I will explain. Liberal education seeks to develop liberal skills, liberal arts within a student. These liberal skills or arts are internal in their purpose and direction; that is, the aim is not to produce some artifact or product external to the maker; the aim of liberal education is to make the student a disciplined person, with skills of the mind and character akin to the physical skills of a pole vaulter or a ballet dancer or a tightrope walker. Liberal education aims to develop the skills of the human psyche, to make us aware of its extraordinary range of abilities—which means a greatly increased capability for understanding, for achievement, for happiness, and, alas, for misery and sorrow too. Liberal education is so named for its power to liberate the human psyche from the fetters of ignorance, superstition, fear, greed, and other follies that tend to enslave human beings, to diminish us, to make us less than we are capable of being.

Let me explain why I use the word "psyche," originally, of course, a Greek word. Whatever psyche is, it is what psychology studies and psychiatry treats. Psyche is sometimes translated from the Greek as mind, sometimes as soul, sometimes as spirit. We moderns are in the strange position of putting great faith in psychology and psychiatry while doubting the existence of the psyche. We eat soul food, listen to soul music, speak of people as lacking soul or having soul—but doubt the existence of the soul. We sing spirituals, have spirited conversations, celebrate the Spirit of '76—but doubt the existence of the human spirit. We are not sure that anything really exists that is not wholly composed of matter.

That is what we mean when we acknowledge that we are materialistic, and materialism is another reason why liberal education—the education that seeks to liberate the psyche—is in danger. Psyche is not exactly the same as soul, not exactly the same as mind, and not exactly the same as spirit, but psyche is everything that we human beings are that is not wholly physical, material, matter, body. Those who are convinced that there is nothing that is not matter, and their numbers are great, are unlikely to be strong advocates and defenders of liberal education, which exists to give freedom to the psyche.

If liberal education is not defined by the subjects studied, how can we define it? Surely every one of us has taken a course usually considered a part of liberal education and found that it not only did not free our psyche but put it into a state of numbness. Great dramas, wonderful poetry—Shakespeare himself—can be taught in such a way that any human being feels himself being enslaved, feels the handcuffs and ankle chains tightening, and realizes that boredom can be so severe as to make one long for death. Why should such activity be called liberal education?

Less common is that rare encounter with the master teacher who can guide us to uncover deep meaning in the activity of shaping pieces of wood or a lump of clay or even a bunch of flowers. When I speak of deep meaning I do not mean that we see it in the wood or the clay or the flowers. No, we see it in ourselves. Why should such activity not be called liberal education?

If I am right, almost any learning effort can be liberalizing or stultifying, and the decisive thing will be not the name of the course but the aim of the effort and whether it develops a skill that liberates the psyche a little or a lot.

When my third daughter, the National Merit finalist, was studying mathematics, languages, literature, history, and sciences at one of the nation's most renowned high schools, I think the most liberating teacher she had was the man who taught her the skills of horsemanship, after school. I am not sure she would agree, but his instruction seemed to affect her psyche and her understanding of what a human being can accomplish more, and more directly, than her academic studies. But let me give you a better and loftier example, before you begin to get the idea that I am antischool and anti-intellectual, which, properly understood, I definitely am not.

Surprise Endings

Consider analytic geometry: is it part of liberal education? Most people who have studied analytic geometry would say no. It is hard to learn; it is almost always studied for directly practical reasons; it has useful applications in engineering; and few people discover much about their psyche while studying analytic geometry, except that they have less endurance than they need or more than they thought possible.

René Descartes, the great French philosopher, wrote the first book of analytic geometry. (You do not need to be a mathematician to follow what I am about to describe, and there will be no geometrical diagrams.) Descartes's book begins by saying that there is a certain problem of geometry, called the problem of Pappus, that has gone unsolved for more than a thousand years. He describes it and draws the diagram; it takes a page or two just to state the problem. Then he says, now I will show you the power of my new method of geometry: I will solve this thousand-year-old unsolved problem.

Step one: Consider the problem already solved. Step two: How did I do it? In a few pages Descartes leads the reader to an understanding of a new method of mathematical reasoning, analysis. This new problem-solving technique, as we would now call it, starts at the end, with the task complete, and goes backward, breaking it down into parts, that is, analyzing it. Immediately we see what we have always half known. For example, it is easier, after we have made a trip, to describe the route we took, step by step, than it is to lay out the route in advance, especially if we have never been there and even more so if we are not sure where we are going.

Once Descartes developed the method of analysis, it occurred to him, and has occurred to others since, that ancient geometry (Euclidean plane and solid geometry, now called synthetic geometry to distinguish it from analytic geometry) had no visible method of its own but was really analytic geometry disguised. That is, to know how to solve a difficult problem in Euclidean geometry, we may have to see the answer first, see the problem in its entirety, analyze it into its parts, and see how the problem was solved. Descartes suspected that the ancients then erased it from their awareness and proceeded step by step to the solution as if they were approaching it anew, without ever having been there.

That is why Euclidean geometry can be so delightful and also so frustrating: frustrating because we feel we are proceeding blindly, delightful because there are such wonderful surprise endings—*if* we get there. Descartes took away both the frustrations and the delightful surprises—an alteration of the human condition now called modernity.

If you did not follow everything I have just said about analytic geometry, it does not matter. The main point is that analytic geometry can indeed be taught as a liberalizing skill, as a way of lifting and strengthening and enlightening the human psyche, showing what it is for, what it can accomplish, how it can build new worlds, how it can see the unseen and give new shape to the heretofore shapeless.

Only one thing gives more joy than making, and that is the understanding that enables us to make. The great liberators of human beings are the ones who have shown us new ways of making and, more important, new ways of understanding. That is why Descartes ranks as one of the great human benefactors, one of the greatest liberal educators, and why he and the few others like him are to be studied and restudied.

It is not wrong, as I may seem to be saying, to think that there is a connection between liberalizing study and certain subjects, certain books, certain authors. What distinguishes Descartes from most other mathematicians is exactly what I have been describing—the liberalizing dimension of his thought, the skills he can impart to his reader that free the psyche by giving it new power. His geometry can be taught without soul, and horsemanship can be taught with soul, but the greatest treasures of liberal education are there in the greatest works of the greatest minds, and it is no mistake that they are considered the source of human riches, even though few teachers know where the gold is or how to help students prospect for it.

Do you wonder what such thoughts have to do with my present official duties in the White House and the U.S. Department of Defense and what I can possibly contribute to better government? First, let me assure you that I wonder sometimes, too. But, second, and this is my first hint that there is good news, it has been my experience in the world of practical affairs that the higher one goes, the more one finds an awareness of the importance of the *liberal* skills—yes, even in a conservative administration.

I first met many of the people I serve with now when they came to liberal arts seminars I ran at the University of Chicago and Kenyon College, including, among many others, my two present bosses, President Gerald Ford and Secretary of Defense Donald Rumsfeld, then congressmen. The strong urge to understand, to learn more, to get to the bottom of things, to grasp the sources and origins of problems—these are characteristic of the best practical men and women.

I have never met a truly practical person, a real leader and manager of grand enterprises, who regularly reacted to inquiry in the tone of, "That may be all right in theory, Professor, but it won't work in practice." The truly practical leaders know very well how directly and powerfully understanding and action are linked; the deeper the understanding, the more likely it is that action will be effective and will accomplish the desired results.

Good News

That brings me to the good news and the conclusion simultaneously. There is no need to despair for liberal education's future: as long as there are human beings, they will never cease their efforts to understand. That is what liberal education is—the effort, the striving, the struggle to understand.

It is not true of all of us or perhaps even of most of us (however we may try to show how "practical" we are) that we will exert ourselves only if there is some monetary or material reward. In fact, we human beings will go to the greatest lengths, against terrible odds, at the risk of sanity and even life, to understand, once we are puzzled; to answer a question, once it begins to bother us; to see more clearly with our mind's eye, once we perceive that there is something there, however dimly glimpsed.

If I am right that the will to understand is a powerful and perhaps irresistible force of human nature, that it cannot be suppressed in some of us even by the fiercest repression, and that it can be awakened in most of us, at least to some extent, by the right kind of questioning, then it is also clear that what we call liberal education is human education, perhaps the only education, surely the education most akin to our nature. I conclude that the future of liberal education is inseparable from, and perhaps even identical to the future of humanity itself.

Notes

Chapter 1: Principles and Politics—An Introduction

1. Gilbert Chinard, *Thomas Jefferson, the Apostle of Americanism*, 2d ed. (Ann Arbor: The University of Michigan Press, 1957), pp. 71–72.
2. *Basic Writings of Thomas Jefferson*, ed. Philip S. Foner (New York: Willey Book Company, 1944), p. 802.
3. Alexander Hamilton, James Madison, and John Jay, *The Federalist*, ed. Clinton Rossiter (New York: New American Library, 1961), No. 14.
4. *The Federalist*, No. 1.

Chapter 2: Why Blacks, Women, and Jews Are Not Mentioned in the Constitution

1. *Constitutional Controversies*, ed. Robert A. Goldwin, William A. Schambra, and Art Kaufman (Washington, D.C.: American Enterprise Institution, 1987), pp. 101, 104.
2. John Hope Franklin, "The Moral Legacy of the Founding Fathers," *University of Chicago Magazine* (Summer 1975), pp. 10–13.
3. Lino A. Graglia, "How the Constitution Disappeared," *Commentary* (February 1986), p. 23.
4. This factual information is drawn from William Wiecek, " 'The Blessings of Liberty': Slavery in the American Constitutional Order," in Robert A. Goldwin and Art Kaufman, eds., *Slavery and Its Consequences: The Constitution, Equality, and Race* (Washington, D.C.: American Enterprise Institute, 1988), p. 31. Wiecek uses these facts, however, to come to quite opposite conclusions from mine.
5. Luther Martin, "Genuine Information" (delivered to the Maryland legislature, November 29, 1787), in Max Farrand, ed., *The Records of the Federal Convention* (New Haven: Yale University Press, 1937), vol. 3, pp. 210–12.
6. Frederick Douglass, "Fourth of July Oration, July 5, 1852," in Herbert J. Storing, ed., *What Country Have I?* (New York: St. Martin's Press, 1970), p. 37.
7. Morton Borden, *Jews, Turks, and Infidels* (Chapel Hill: University of North Carolina Press, 1984), pp. 11–13.
8. Jacob Rader Marcus, "Introduction," Jacob R. Marcus and Abraham J. Peck, eds., *Jews, Judaism and the American Constitution* (New York: American Jewish Archives, 1982), p. 1.

Chapter 3: Of Men and Angels: A Search for Morality in the Constitution

1. This list was composed in 1977. If it were being written in 1989, the items would be different, but the argument would be unchanged.
2. For those who wish to ponder this subject more thoroughly, I suggest reading the discussions of salary for public officials in *The Records of the Federal Convention of 1787*, 4 vols., ed. Max Farrand, (New Haven: Yale University

Press, 1911–37). See Index: salaries of congressmen, salary of executive, salary of judges. See also *The Federalist*, No. 72.

3. John Locke, *Two Treatises of Government* (Cambridge, England: Cambridge University Press, 1960), ed. Peter Laslett. Book 2, section 90.

4. Aristotle, *Nicomachean Ethics*, Book 2, 1103b. There is, of course, no indication in the Greek text that the word *Constitution* is capitalized.

5. *The Federalist*, No. 51.

6. "Newton and the Liberal Arts," *The College*, January 1976, St. John's College, Annapolis, Md.

7. Alexis de Tocqueville, *Democracy in America* (New York: Harper and Row, 1966), p. 223.

8. As for Dr. Simpson's contention that the Constitution is drawn out of mathematical insight, this comment of Aristotle's should suffice: "A carpenter and a geometrician both seek after a right angle, but in different ways" (*Nicomachean Ethics*, Book 1, 1098a).

Chapter 7: Rights versus Duties

1. *The Federalist*, No. 51, p. 322. According to Locke, once a civil society is established, it may be said to acquire a life of its own, and then, "acting according to its own nature," it acts for "the preservation of the community" (*Two Treatises of Government*, Book II, section 149). In this way the "public rights" Madison speaks of also have self-preservation as their rock-bottom starting point.

2. *The Federalist*, No. 51, p. 324.

3. Ibid., No. 10, p. 79.

4. Ibid., p. 81.

5. Ibid., No. 51, p. 322.

6. *The New Soviet Constitution of 1977: Analysis and Text*, analysis by Robert Sharlet (Brunswick, Ohio: King's Court Communications, 1978), pp. 89–96.

7. Ibid., p. 89.

8. *The Federalist*, No. 51, p. 322.

9. I first heard the phrase "moral greed" from Lady Jacqueline Wheldon, the English novelist and playwright.

Chapter 10: A Reading of Locke's Chapter "Of Property"

1. Henry Hallam, *Introduction to the Literature of Europe in the Fifteenth, Sixteenth and Seventeenth Centuries*, vol. 4 (London: John Murray, 1839), p. 203.

2. All references in the text are to sections of the *Second Treatise*. I have followed the text, punctuation, and spelling of the Laslett edition, but not the capitalization or italicization. Hereafter references not otherwise identified are to the *Two Treatises*.

3. *Some Considerations of the Lowering of Interest and Raising the Value of Money*, in *The Works of John Locke in Nine Volumes* vol. 4, pp. 40–41. (12th ed. (London, 1824).

4. The Latin text and English translation of this passage appear in John Locke, *Essays on the Law of Nature,* ed. W. von Leyden (Oxford: Clarendon, 1954), pp. 210, 211; some minor revisions of the translation were provided by Leo Strauss. Reprinted by permission of Oxford University Press.

5. Ibid., p. 213.

6. *Second Treatise,* sec. 42. This passage is one of the most important of those added by Locke in the last version he corrected. It does not appear in many editions now available and is misprinted in several editions in which it does appear. It is erroneously printed as "the increase of lands and the right of employing of them," rather than the correct text, "the increase of lands and the right employing of them." Examination of the handwritten text leaves no doubt that the superfluous "of" is a printer's error, with what distortion of the meaning of the passage the attentive reader will readily see.

Chapter 11: Locke's State of Nature in Political Society

1. R. Ashcraft, "Locke's State of Nature: Historical Fact or Moral Fiction?" *American Political Science Review,* vol. 62 (September 1968), pp. 898–915, an article remarkable for its scholarly obscurity and superficiality.

2. II, secs. 4, 3.

3. II, secs. 4, 7.

4. II, sec. 19.

5. II, sec. 6.

6. II, sec. 13.

7. II, sec. 20.

8. II, sec. 19.

9. Thomas Hobbes, *De Cive,* "The Author's Preface to the Reader"; chap. 5, art. 2.

10. II, sec. 19.

11. II, sec. 212.

12. II, sec. 14; cf. sec. 184.

13. Ibid.

14. II, sec. 19.

15. Ibid.; cf. sec. 207.

16. Ibid.

17. II, sec. 17.

18. For a discussion of a use of "scatter'd" writing, see I, secs. 7ff.

19. I, sec. 86.

20. I, sec. 88.

21. II, sec. 124; cf. II, sec. 12, Locke's reference to "a studier of that law."

22. II, sec. 135.

23. II, sec. 7.

24. II, secs. 7, 8ff.

25. II, sec. 16.

26. II, sec. 7.

27. II, sec. 8.

28. Ibid.

29. II, sec. 11.
30. II, sec. 16.
31. Ibid.
32. II, secs. 6, 7, 8, 11, 16.
33. II, sec. 171.
34. II, secs. 16, 8.
35. II, sec. 13.
36. Hobbes, *Leviathan*, chap. 13.
37. Hobbes, *De Cive*, "Author's Preface to the Reader."
38. Ibid., chap. 5, art. 2.
39. II, sec. 87.
40. II, secs. 128, 130.
41. II, sec. 128.
42. II, sec. 129.
43. II, sec. 130.
44. II, sec. 87.
45. II, sec. 88.
46. II, sec. 171.
47. II, sec. 168.
48. II, secs. 128, 129, 202, 222.
49. II, chap. iv, esp. sec. 23; cf. II, sec. 85.
50. II, sec. 90; cf. "The Preface."
51. II, sec. 91. Note Locke's distinction of "the ordinary state of nature" and "the unrestrained state of nature."
52. II, secs. 209, 210, 225, 230.
53. II, sec. 137.

Chapter 13: Common Sense versus "The Common Heritage"

1. "The creation of the International Seabed Authority by the consensus of practically the entire world community (in which the consent of the U.S. must be counted, because it was given at the Conference *and will, I am sure, be given again*) . . ." (emphasis added). Elisabeth Mann Borgese, "The Law of the Sea," *Scientific American* (March 1983), pp. 42–49.

2. "Does President Reagan know what he is doing in preparing a final decision not to sign the law of the sea treaty?" *Washington Post*, editorial, July 9, 1982.

3. "The guardians of pure conservative ideology may have won a battle when the United States stood alone at the Law of the Sea Conference, but the United States may lose a very important war." Leigh Ratiner, "The Law of the Sea: A Crossroads for American Foreign Policy," *Foreign Affairs*, vol. 60 (Summer 1982), p. 1020.

4. "If President Reagan understood the realistic prospects . . . he would have had second thoughts about the pursuit of principle over pragmatism." Ibid., p. 1018. Discourse on this subject has rarely been dispassionate and often descends to vituperative name calling. A comparatively mild example

appeared as a column in the *New York Times* by Clifton E. Curtis, identified as an attorney with the Center for Law and Social Policy; in it Curtis characterized the Reagan administration as "jingoistic ideologues" suffering from "ideological paranoia," who "should be deep-sixed." The title of his column is the imperious command "Sign the Sea Law Treaty," *New York Times*, February 21, 1983, p. A17. Curtis is professionally concerned with control of ocean pollution, but he seems less concerned about the consequences of polluting rational discourse.

5. Statement by the president, July 9, 1982, White House, Office of the Press Secretary (Santa Barbara, Calif.).

6. For a full discussion of "the common heritage of mankind" as an ideological doctrine and the theoretical errors it has led to in the Law of the Sea Treaty negotiations, see "Locke and the Law of the Sea," chap. 12 in this volume.

7. I, unfortunately, was not one of them, relying as I did on what others were saying about the factual matters. See my references to resources "worth billions of dollars" and how the world "suffers from a shortage of these metals," in ibid.

8. "Manganese Nodule Mining: Background Information," submitted to the Special Standing Committee of the House of Commons on the Deep Sea Mining (Temporary Provisions) Bill by Consolidated Gold Fields Limited, Rio Tinto-Zinc Corporation Limited, and BP Petroleum Development Limited, May 1981. Other members of the Kennecott Consortium are Kennecott Corporation (United States), Mitsubishi Corporation (Japan), and Noranda Mines Limited (Canada).

9. Reported in *Financial Times* (London), October 6, 1982, p. 26.

10. "Minesweeping," *Economist* (London), December 11, 1982, p. 60.

11. Hobart Rowen, "The Ceramic Example," *Washington Post*, February 17, 1983, p. A19.

12. "Manganese Nodule Mining: Background Information."

13. "Declining commodity prices made the resource-exporting developing countries wary of a new source of competition for their native ones. Against the opposition of the North (with the exception of Canada) these countries became more interested in limiting production from the seabed than in managing it." Borgese, "The Law of the Sea," p. 47.

14. C. R. Tinsley, "The Financing of Deep-Sea Mining" (Paper prepared for a conference on U.S. Interests in the Law of the Sea, American Enterprise Institute, October 1981).

15. "There exists no politician in India daring enough to attempt to explain to the masses that cows can be eaten." Indira Gandhi, talking to Oriana Fallaci, quoted in *The Quotable Woman, 1800–1981*, ed. Elaine Partnow; from a book review by Edmund Fuller, *Wall Street Journal*, March 28, 1983, p. 22.

16. Borgese, "The Law of the Sea," p. 47.

17. International diplomats in the United Nations, sad to say, continue their efforts on behalf of the principle of "the common heritage of mankind," despite their setback on the Law of the Sea Treaty. See the introduction to this volume.

Acknowledgments

CHAPTER 2, "WHY BLACKS, WOMEN, AND JEWS ARE NOT MENTIONED IN THE CONSTITUTION," is reprinted from *Commentary*, vol. 83, no. 5 (May 1987).

CHAPTER 3, "OF MEN AND ANGELS: A SEARCH FOR MORALITY IN THE CONSTITUTION," first appeared in Robert Horwitz, ed., *The Moral Foundations of the American Republic* (Charlottesville, Va.: University of Virginia Press, 1977). Reprinted with permission.

CHAPTER 4, "HOW THE CONSTITUTION PROMOTES PROGRESS," first appeared in a shorter version under the title "Keeping Those Ideas Coming," in THINK Magazine, vol. 53, no. 4 (September 1987). Reprinted by permission. Copyright 1987. International Business Machines Corporation.

CHAPTER 5, "WHAT AMERICANS KNOW ABOUT THEIR CONSTITUTION," first appeared under the title "Amending the Record: What Americans Know about the Constitution," in *Public Opinion* (September/October 1987).

CHAPTER 6, "IS THERE AN AMERICAN RIGHT OF REVOLUTION?" was originally presented as a lecture at Colgate University to celebrate the bicentennial of the Declaration of Independence, July 2, 1976.

CHAPTER 7, "RIGHTS VERSUS DUTIES," first appeared under the title "Rights versus Duties: No Contest," in Arthur L. Caplan and Daniel Callahan, eds., *Ethics in Hard Times* (New York: Plenum Press, 1981). Reprinted with permission.

CHAPTER 8, "ARE HUMAN RIGHTS THE MORAL FOUNDATION OF AMERICAN FOREIGN POLICY?" first appeared under the title "Human Rights: The Moral Foundation for American Foreign Policy," in Jeffrey Salmon, ed., *Power, Principles and Interests: A Reader in World Politics* (Chicago: Loyola University of Chicago, 1978). Reprinted by permission of the Institute for Political Philosophy and Policy Analysis, Department of Political Science, Loyola University of Chicago.

CHAPTER 9, "THREE HUMAN RIGHTS ARE ENOUGH," is reprinted, by permission, from *The Center Magazine* (July/August 1984).

CHAPTER 10, "A READING OF LOCKE'S CHAPTER 'OF PROPERTY,' " is reprinted from Leo Strauss and Joseph Cropsey, eds., *History of Political Philosophy* (Chicago: University of Chicago Press, 1963; 3d ed., 1987). Reprinted by permission of the University of Chicago Press.

CHAPTER 11, "LOCKE'S STATE OF NATURE IN POLITICAL SOCIETY," is reprinted, by permission, from *Western Political Quarterly,* vol. 29, no. 1 (March 1976).

CHAPTER 12, "LOCKE AND THE LAW OF THE SEA," is reprinted from *Commentary,* vol. 71, no. 6 (June 1981).

CHAPTER 13, "COMMON SENSE VERSUS 'THE COMMON HERITAGE,'" first appeared in Bernard H. Oxman et al., eds., *Law of the Sea: U.S. Policy Dilemma* (San Francisco: Institute for Contemporary Studies Press, 1983).

CHAPTER 14, "PRESCRIPTION FOR SUPPRESSING A DREADFUL THOUGHT," was a commencement address at New College, Sarasota, Florida, June 11, 1977.

CHAPTER 15, "LEARNING TO EARN A LIVING AND LEARNING TO LIVE A LIFE," was a commencement address at Virginia Wesleyan University, May 21, 1977.

CHAPTER 16, "THE FUTURE OF LIBERAL EDUCATION," is reprinted, by permission, from the *Education Record,* vol. 57, no. 2, © 1976 by the American Council on Education, Washington, D.C. The first version was a speech at the Academy-Business-Community Forum, University of Nebraska May 5, 1976. At the time, the author was special consultant to the president of the United States and adviser to the U.S. secretary of defense.

Index

About the Author

ROBERT A. GOLDWIN is a resident scholar and director of constitutional studies at the American Enterprise Institute in Washington, D.C. He has taught political science at the University of Chicago and Kenyon College and was dean of St. John's College in Annapolis, Maryland.

He served in the White House during the Ford administration as special consultant to the president, in the Pentagon as adviser to the secretary of defense, and in Brussels as special adviser to the U.S. ambassador to NATO.

Editor or co-editor of more than a score of books on American politics, Mr. Goldwin has also written numerous articles in journals and magazines on human rights, higher education, political philosophy, the law of the sea, and the Constitution of the United States. Among the books he has co-edited at AEI are *How Democratic Is the Constitution?*, *How Capitalistic Is the Constitution?*, and *How Does the Constitution Protect Religious Freedom?*

He received a Guggenheim Fellowship, the Professional Achievement Award from the University of Chicago, the Award for Outstanding Service from the U.S. Information Agency, the Medal for Distinguished Public Service from the Department of Defense, and honorary doctorates from Kenyon College and Marietta College.

He earned his bachelor's degree from St. John's College and his master's and doctor's degrees in political science from the University of Chicago.

A NOTE ON THE BOOK

*This book was edited by Trudy Kaplan,
Dana Lane, and Janet Schilling of the
publications staff of the American Enterprise Institute.
The index was prepared by Patricia Ruggiero.
The text was set in Palatino, a typeface designed by Hermann Zapf.
Coghill Composition Company, of Richmond, Virginia,
set the type, and Edwards Brothers Incorporated,
of Ann Arbor, Michigan, printed and bound the book,
using permanent acid-free paper.*

The AEI Press is the publisher for the American Enterprise Institute for Public Policy Research, 1150 17th Street, N.W., Washington, D.C. 20036: *Christopher C. DeMuth,* publisher; *Edward Styles,* director; *Dana Lane,* editor; *Ann Petty,* editor; *Andrea Posner,* editor; *Teresa Fung,* editorial assistant (rights and permissions). Books published by the AEI Press are distributed by arrangement with the University Press of America, 4720 Boston Way, Lanham, Md. 20706.